ENGLYNION Y BEDDAU
THE STANZAS OF THE GRAVES

Pentre Ifan Neolithic burial chamber, Pembrokeshire

Englynion y Beddau
The Stanzas of the Graves

Verses on the Legendary Heroes of Wales from
The Black Book of Carmarthen

EDITED AND TRANSLATED BY
JOHN K BOLLARD

PHOTOGRAPHS BY
ANTHONY GRIFFITHS

First edition: 2015
Copyright © text: John K. Bollard, 2015
Copyright © photographs: Anthony Griffiths, 2015

John K. Bollard and Anthony Griffiths have asserted their rights under the Copyright, Design and Patents Act, 1988, to be identified as the joint-authors of this Work.

All rights reserved No part of this book may be reproduced, stored in a retrieval system, or transmitted in any form or by any means, electronic, electrostatic, magnetic tape, mechanical, photocopying, recording or otherwise, without permission of the publishers:

Gwasg Carreg Gwalch
12 Iard yr Orsaf, Llanrwst, Dyffryn Conwy, Cymru LL26 0EH.
Tel: 01492 642031 Fax: 01492 641502 Email: llanrwst@carreg-gwalch.com

ISBN: 978-1-84527-509-9

A CIP record for this title is available from the British Library.

Cover and book design: Eleri Owen

The publisher acknowledges the financial support of the Welsh Books Council.

Printed and bound in Wales by Gwasg Cambrian, Aberystwyth, Ceredigion, SY23 3TN

Black Book of Carmarthen, fol. 32 photo, p. 8, courtesy of the National Library of Wales.

Parc y Meirch hoard photo, p. 48, courtesy of the National Museum of Wales.

The map on p. 15 contains Ordnance Survey data
© Crown copyright and database right.

We acknowledge the use of material from Professor Melville Richards's place-name research archive deposited at the University of Wales Bangor, accessed through the Archif Melville Richards database (AMR), a project funded by grants from the University of Wales Board of Celtic Studies and the Arts and Humanities Research Board.

COVER PHOTOS by ANTHONY GRIFFITHS
Pentre Ifan Neolitic burial chamber, Pembrokeshire (front)
Sunset at Maen Dylan, Caernarfonshire (rear)

Er cof am | *In memory of*

Joan Griffiths
Ruth E. Bollard

Contents

Foreword	9
Photographer's Notes	13
Key to the Map and a Note on the Texts	14
A Map of Locations	15
Englynion y Beddau | The Stanzas of the Graves	17
Notes and Commentary	60
Afterword: The Text and Context of Englynion y Beddau	109
A Brief Note on Metre	126
Textual Notes	128
Abbreviations and Bibliography	133
Index of Personal Names	137
Index of Place Names	142

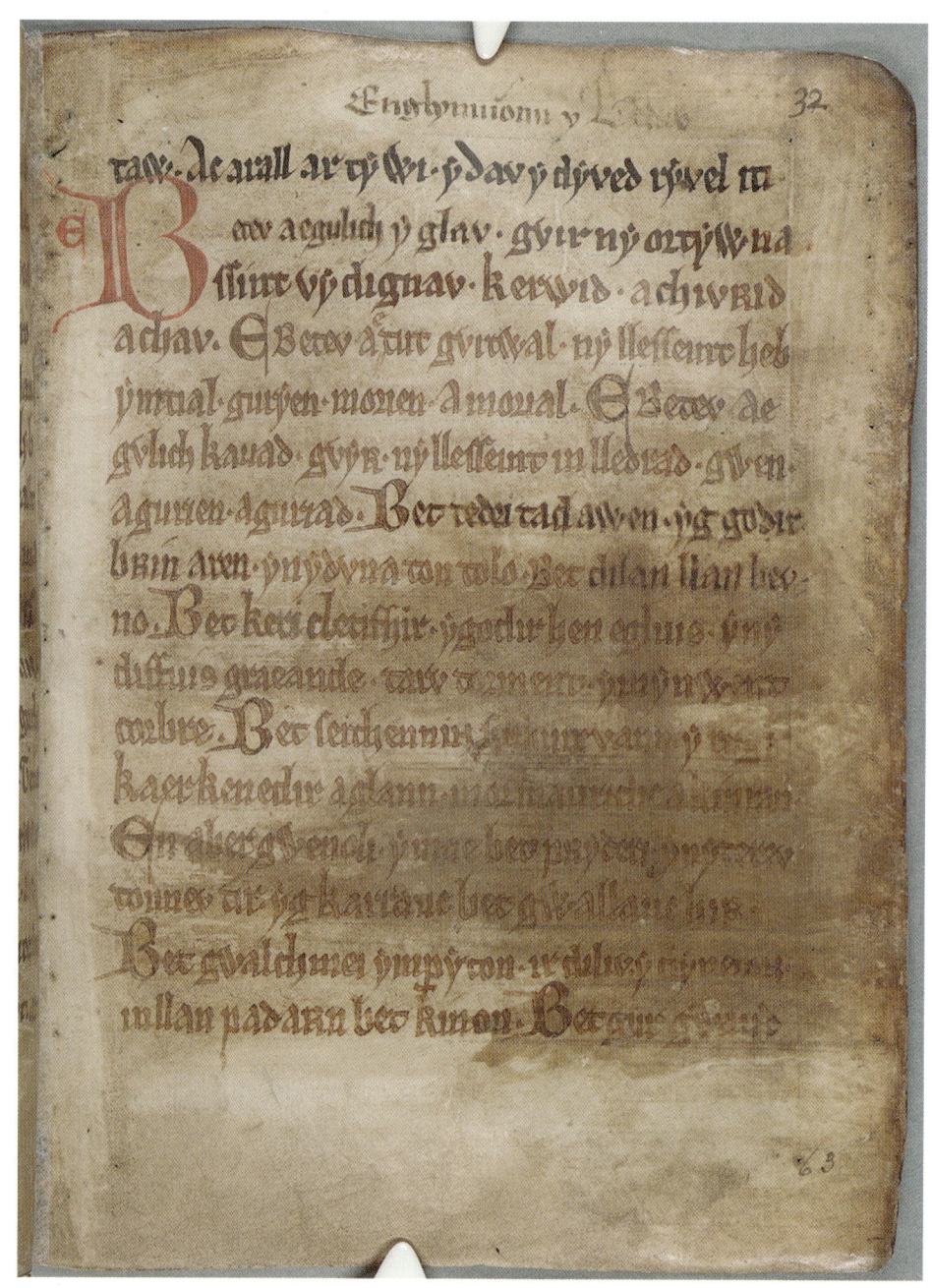

The Black Book of Carmarthen, folio 32a

Foreword
John K. Bollard

Englynion y Beddau | *The Stanzas of the Graves* is a series of stanzas that name about ninety legendary Welsh heroes and identify many of their grave sites. Despite, or perhaps because of, their apparent simplicity, these seventy-three stanzas in traditional englyn form have fascinated and intrigued readers for centuries – even, we might hazard to say, since they were first copied into the famous *Black Book of Carmarthen*, the earliest surviving book of Welsh poetry, in the mid thirteenth century. Both the language and subject matter suggest that they were composed considerably earlier, perhaps in the ninth or tenth century. While scholars have frequently turned to the text for information about the heroes who are named or about the places in which they are said to be buried, the poetry has not, to any significant degree, been much studied or appreciated.

The text is presented here both in modernized Welsh spelling and in close English translation to encourage readers to approach these stanzas as they might read any poem – with an open mind and the assumption that the poet has a purpose beyond conveying information that could be presented more easily in prose. In addition to the text in the *Black Book*, this book includes texts and translations of grave stanzas found in the late fourteenth-century *Red Book of Hergest*, in the early seventeenth-century National Library of Wales Peniarth MS 98B, and a single stanza in the late sixteenth-century Wrexham MS 1. The English versions given here are not meant as a poetic rendering of the Welsh; they simply attempt to convey as clearly as I can the meaning of the original as I understand it. Thus, even readers who do not speak or read Welsh might want to look carefully at the Welsh text to get some sense of the richness of rhythm, rhyme, alliteration, and assonance that raises this poetry above the level of everyday speech.

The text and translation are followed by notes and commentary on the names and places in each stanza. Readers who might want an introduction to the text before reading it might like to turn first to the essay on *'The Text and Context of Englynion y Beddau'* on page 109.

The photographs accompanying the text illustrate the landscape within which the lore embedded in the poetry was preserved. Many of the places named in the text cannot be identified with any certainty, but the ones that can are scattered across all of Wales. This alone shows that even though Wales was not politically united there was an awareness of both Wales and Welshness as a coherent cultural unity. The names and traditions of ancient heroes from *yr Hen Ogledd*, 'the Old North' of northern England and southern Scotland, were relocated in Wales and became important in establishing a Welsh sense of deep history and identity as a people. The places to which those names became attached, often mysterious prehistoric cromlechs, tumuli, standing stones, and other otherwise inexplicable remains in the landscape, came to serve as the physical evidence testifying to that history and to the fact that the land is indeed the land of the *Cymry*, 'those who live together in this region'.

I have been extremely fortunate to have Anthony Griffiths as a partner once again in conceiving and realizing this book. He has trekked through bog and brake to capture the beauty, the mystery, and the history of the Welsh landscape, and his photographs bring the *Stanzas of the Graves* off the page and into our visual imaginations. His artistry is evident throughout these pages – his dedication and tenacity are reflected in this impromptu account of the search for the Parc Maen Llwyd standing stone illustrated on p. 98:

> We wandered across a marsh, behind a row of houses in Puncheston. No sign of stone! Child in back garden had never heard of it. The local school was closing so I asked a teacher, who had also never heard of the stone but said the couple getting out of their car opposite had lived in the village a long time and might know about it. Yes, the man said it's in the garden of the house right over there! At the house, the lady was most helpful and took us into the back garden. Very impressive standing stone, surrounded by sheds, glasshouses, washing lines, bird feeders, flower pots, and a fish pond!

I owe a doubly great debt to the late Professor Thomas Jones, whose groundbreaking edition of these stanzas paved the way for the present book and who introduced me to the serious study of early Welsh literature. Many thanks, too, go to Professor Gwyn Thomas, who read the entire text with great care, correcting errors with a scholar's eye and improving the translation with a poet's ear. Numerous friends and colleagues have provided invaluable help and encouragement along the way, and have listened patiently as this work developed. Among these I must mention David Austin, Dafydd Johnston, Gruffudd Aled Williams, Patrick Sims-Williams, Marged Haycock, William Oram, John Dolven, Henry Lyman, and especially Brynley Lloyd-Bollard and Catrin Lloyd-Bollard. Our publisher, Myrddin ap Dafydd, has done a wonderful job shepherding this work through the press, and the book's designer, Eleri Owen, has transformed a difficult complex of texts and photos into an elegant volume. We are grateful to Jen Llywelyn for preparing a grant proposal and to the Welsh Books Council for awarding the grant which made this book possible. Thanks to the National Library of Wales for providing the photograph of folio 32a of the *Black Book of Carmarthen* and to the National Museum of Wales for the photograph of the Parc y Meirch hoard. My profoundest thanks, as always, go to my wife, Margaret Lloyd, whose faith in me and in this work has been unwavering.

Florence, Massachusetts

Foel Feddau ('bare hill of graves'), Mynydd Preseli, with Foel Drygarn in the middle distance, Frenni Fawr beyond, and Carn Menyn to the right

St P3. Morfa Dinlle, looking south towards the hills of northern Llŷn

Photographer's Notes
Anthony Griffiths

This, my fourth book with John Bollard, has been a departure from the previous ones. With the exception of a few slides, most of the photographs were taken digitally, and they have not been altered with Photoshop. Like many photographers I thought I'd be the last person to "go over" to digital, but "gone over" I have, and I am pleased with the results.

My camera is a Nikon D90, with a 16-85mm lens. I use a polarizer and a graduated neutral density filter.

Working on the *Stanzas* took us along the banks of many little-known Welsh streams in remote valleys. It was especially rewarding re-discovering the Brwyno stone alignment. Almost impossible to locate inside the edge of a forestry plantation, it now stands in what would have been, in the Bronze Age, a magnificent location on a ridge overlooking the Dyfi estuary with splendid views north to the mountains of Snowdonia, and Llŷn.

I looked forward to returning to Llŷn and the Dinas Dinlle area, much celebrated in the Fourth Branch of *The Mabinogi*. This part of north-west Wales is very beautiful and held fond memories for my mother, who camped at Morfa Dinlle in her youth. It was a memorable visit – towards evening the clouds lifted from Yr Eifl as we walked along the shore of Morfa Dinlle in the sunset.

I would like to thank the landowners and farmers who were extremely helpful and obliging when visiting their land. Finally, thanks to my wife Marjorie, who has been an invaluable help working on this book with me.

Aberystwyth

Map of sites named in Englynion y Beddau | The Stanzas of the Graves

The map on the facing page illustrates the wide geographical distribution throughout Wales of sites named in *Englynion y Beddau*. Stanza numbers, as given in the text (e.g., 4, P7, R2), indicate the approximate location of a site mentioned in that stanza. Not all stanzas are represented, because some do not include place names and because some place names can not be located. While many of the site identifications are uncertain, some of the more tentative locations, as well as names with more than one possible location (e.g., 54), are followed by a question mark. Some numbers appear more than once because a stanza names two places. For example, St 8 names both Llanbadarn, probably Llanbadarn Fawr in Ceredigion, and Peryddon, for which two possible locations are marked on the map.

A Note on the Texts

The original texts of *The Stanzas of the Graves* are here presented in modern Welsh spelling. A few exceptions are made in cases where the modern spelling would obscure the original rhyming pattern, as in St(anza) 45, where *i danaw* and *ei gwynaw* preserve the early rhyme with *glaw* that *i dano* and *ei gwyno* would mask. Where the manuscript readings make grammatical and logical sense the text has not usually been emended, even where a line seems to have too many or too few syllables. The syllabic constraints of such early englynion were not as sharply delineated as they became in later centuries, and it seems better to present readers with the texts as we have them, mentioning possible emendations in the notes. For example, in St 38, *Beidog Rudd yw hwn, mab Emyr Llydaw* would scan better if we delete *yw hwn* (is this); however, the manuscript reading is grammatically sound. This reading may reflect, if not the original line, the scribe's thought as he wrote it, allowing us for a very brief moment to participate in his personal engagement with the poem as he unconsciously completes the syntax.

CYMRU | WALES

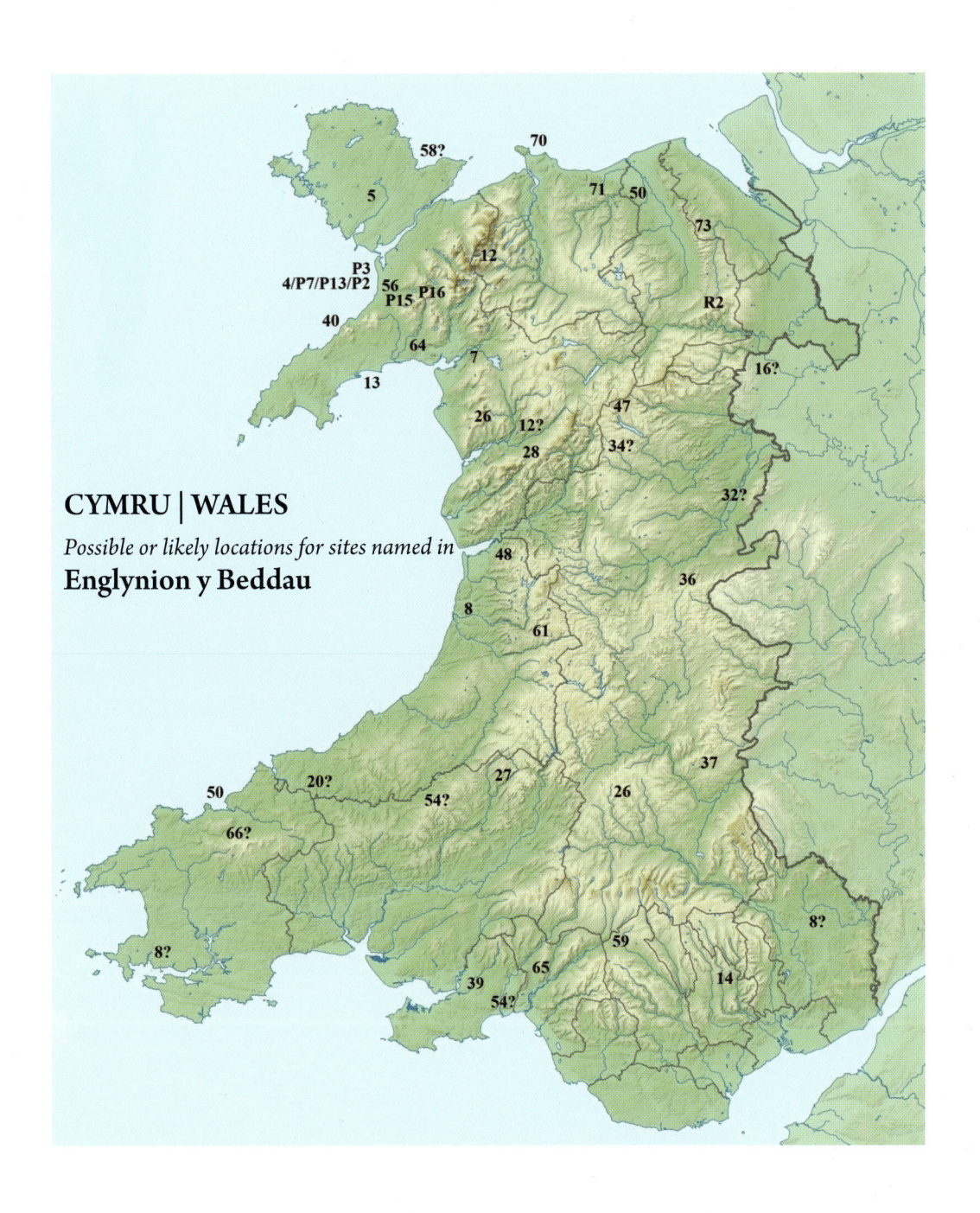

Possible or likely locations for sites named in
Englynion y Beddau

St 4. Maen Dylan, with Dinas Dinlle (St P3) on the horizon to the right

ENGLYNION Y BEDDAU
I. Llyfr Du Caerfyrddin

Y beddau a'u gwlych y glaw –
gwŷr ni orddyfnasynt hwy ddignaw:
Cerwyd a Chywryd a Chaw.

Y beddau a'u tud gwyddwal –
ni llesaint heb ymddial:
Gwrien, Morien, a Morial.

Y beddau a'u gwlych cawad –
gwŷr ni llesaint yn lledrad:
Gwên a Gwrien a Gwriad.

Bedd Tydai Tad Awen
yng ngodir Bryn Aren.
Yn ydd wna ton tolo –
bedd Dylan Llanfeuno.

THE STANZAS OF THE GRAVES
I. The Black Book of Carmarthen

1   The graves which the rain wets –
    men who were not used to being offended:
    Cerwyd and Cywryd and Caw.

2   The graves which the thicket covers –
    they were not slain unavenged:
    Gwrien, Morien, and Morial.

3   The graves which a shower wets –
    men who were not slain by stealth:
    Gwên and Gwrien and Gwriad.

4   The grave of Tydai, Father of Poetry,
    in the lowland of Bryn Arien.
    Where the wave makes noise –
    the grave of Dylan at Llanfeuno.

Bedd Ceri Cleddyf Hir yng ngodir Heneglwys,
    yn y diffwys graeandde,
    tarw torment, ym mynwent Corbre.

5 *The grave of Ceri Long-sword in the lowland of Heneglwys,*
    on the gravelly slopes,
    bull of a host, in Corbre's burial ground.

*St 5. Mynwent Corbre and the church of
St Llwydian, Heneglwys, Anglesey*

Bedd Seithennin synnwyr fan
i rwng Caer Genedr a glan
môr, mawrhydig a gynran.

6 *The grave of Seithennin of lofty wisdom,
between Caer Genedr and the shore
of the sea, a magnificent leader.*

*St 6. The sunken forest of Cantre'r Gwaelod,
between Borth and Ynyslas, inundated through Seithennin's negligence*

Yn Aber Gwenoli
y mae bedd Pryderi.
Yn y tery tonnau tir
yng Ngarrog – bedd Gwallog Hir.

7 *At Aber Gwenoli*
is the grave of Pryderi.
Where the waves strike the land
at Carrog – the grave of Gwallog the Tall.

St 7. Afon Carrog, near Morfa Dinlle

St 7. Aber Gwenoli, near Maentwrog

Bedd Gwalchmai ym Mheryddon	8	*The grave of Gwalchmai in Peryddon,*
yr dilyw i ddyneddon.		*as a disgrace to men.*
Yn Llanbadarn – bedd Cynon.		*In Llanbadarn – the grave of Cynon.*

St 8. Sandyhaven Pill (Peryddon?), Pembrokeshire

St 8. Nant Gern (Peryddon?)
entering the Monnow, north of Monmouth

Bedd gŵr gwawd urddyn, yn uchel dyddyn,
    yn isel gwelyddyn –
  bedd Cynon ap Clydno Eidyn.

Bedd Rhun ap Pyd yn Ergryd afon,
    yn oerfel, yng ngweryd.
  Bedd Cynon yn Rheon Rhyd.

Piau'r bedd i dan y bryn?
Bedd gŵr gwrdd yng nghynisgyn –
bedd Cynon ap Clydno Eidyn.

Bedd mab Osfran yng Nghamlan
gwedi llawer cyflafan.
Bedd Bedwyr yn allt Tryfan.

9   *The grave of a man honored in verse, in a high dwelling,*
      in a low bed –
    the grave of Cynon ap Clydno Eidyn.

10 *The grave of Rhun ap Pyd on the river Ergryd,*
      in the cold, in the earth.
    The grave of Cynon at Rheon Ford.

11 *Whose is the grave under the hill?*
    The grave of a man fierce in attack –
    the grave of Cynon ap Clydno Eidyn.

12 *The grave of Osfran's son at Camlan*
    after much battle.
    The grave of Bedwyr on the slope of Tryfan.

St 12. Camlan at Mallwyd, south-east of Dolgellau

St 12. Allt Tryfan, in the Glyderau Range, Snowdonia

Bedd Owain ab Urien ym mhedryael byd
    dan weryd Llanforfael.
  Yn Abererch – Rhydderch Hael.

Gwedi gwrm a choch a chain
a gorfyddawr mawr mynrhain –
yn Llan Heledd, bedd Owain.

Gwedi gweli a gwaedlan
a gwisgo seirch a meirch can,
neud ef hwn bedd Cynddylan.

13   The grave of Owain son of Urien in a four-sided world
    under the earth of Llanforfael.
  At Abererch – Rhydderch the Generous.

14   After blue and red and fair
and great strong-necked steeds –
at Llanhiledd, the grave of Owain.

15   After a wound and a bloody field
and wearing armour and white steeds,
this is the grave of Cynddylan.

St 13. A lone standing stone on the shore at Abererch, on the Llŷn peninsula

St 14. A Norman motte, possibly built over a prehistoric burial site at Llanhiledd

St 14. St. Illtyd's Church, Llanhiledd, Monmouthshire

Piau'r bedd, da ei gystlwn, a wnai ar Loegr lu cynghrwn? Bedd Gwên ap Llywarch hwn.	16 Whose is the grave, good his kinship, who would take a close-ranked host against Lloegr? The grave of Gwên ap Llywarch this.
Piau'r bedd yn yr amgant a'i tud môr a goror nant? Bedd Meigen ap Rhun, rhwyf cant.	17 Whose is the grave in the region which the sea and the edge of the valley cover? The grave of Meigen ap Rhun, lord of a hundred.

St 16. A Bronze Age ring cairn, Selattyn Hill, near Oswestry, traditionally the burial site of Gwên ap Llywarch

Piau'r bedd yn yr ynys
a'e tud môr a goror gwrys?
Bedd Meigen ap Rhun, rhwyf llys.

Ys cul y bedd ac ys hir
yn llwrw lliaws Amir –
Bedd Meigen ap Rhun, rhwyf gwir.

Tri bedd, tri bodog yn ardderchog bryn
    ym Mhant Gwyn Gwynionog –
Môr a Meilyr a Madog.

18   *Whose is the grave in the island*
which the sea and the edge of the thicket cover?
The grave of Meigen ap Rhun, lord of a court.

19   *Narrow is the grave and long*
in the track of Amir's host –
the grave of Meigen ap Rhun, lord of right.

20   *Three graves, three steadfast ones on a prominent hill*
    in Pant-gwyn Gwynionog –
Môr and Meilyr and Madog.

St 20. Foel Drygarn, Pembrokeshire, with its three massive Bronze Age cairns

Bedd Madog, mur eglwg yng nghyflwg cynnen,
 wŷr Urien gorhëwg,
  mab i Wyn o Wynllŵg.
	21 The grave of Madog, a conspicuous bulwark in the midst of battle,
	 the eager descendant of Urien,
	  the son of Gwyn of Gwynllŵg.

Bedd Môr Mawrhydig, diysig unben,
 post cynnen cyntëig,
  mab Peredur Penweddig.
	22 The grave of Môr the Majestic, lively chieftain,
	 swift-moving pillar of conflict,
	  son of Peredur of Penweddig.

Bedd Meilyr Malwynog, salwfodog synnwyr,
 fysgiad ffwyr ffodiog,
  mab i Frwyn o Frycheiniog.
	23 The grave of Meilyr Malwynog, mean-minded by nature,
	 fortunate router of terror,
	  son of Brwyn of Brycheiniog.

St 23. Fan Brycheiniog and Blaentawe

Piau'r bedd yn Rhyd Faen-ced
a'i ben gan yr anwaered?
Bedd Rhun ab Alun Dyfed.

Bedd Alun Dyfed yn ei drefred draw –
   ni chiliai o galed –
  mab Meigen; mad pan aned.

Bedd Llia Gwyddel yn argel Ardudwy
   dan y gwellt a'i gwefel.
  Bedd Epynt yn nyffryn Gefel.

24   *Whose is the grave at Rhyd Faen-ced
with his head downhill?
The grave of Rhun ab Alun Dyfed.*

25   *The grave of Alun Dyfed in his homestead yonder –
he did not retreat from hardship –
Meigen's son; it was fortunate when he was born.*

26   *The grave of Llia the Irishman in the remoteness of Ardudwy
under the grass that hides him.
The grave of Epynt in the Gefail valley.*

St 26. Maen Llia, one of a group of monuments above the Llia valley, north of Ystradfellte

St 26. Nant Gefail at Abergefail on the slopes of Mynydd Epynt

St 26. The Sgethin Valley, Ardudwy

Bedd Dywel ab Erbin yng ngwestedin Caeo,
    ny byddai gŵr i frenhin,
  difai ni ochelai drin.

Bedd Gwrgi gwychydd a Gwyndodydd lew
    a bedd Llawr lluofydd –
  yng ngwarthaf Gwanas Gwŷr y sydd.

27   The grave of Dywel ab Erbin on the plain of Caeo –
    he would not be vassal to a king –
  faultless, he would not avoid battle.

28   The grave of Gwrgi, a hero and a brave Venedotian,
    and the grave of Llawr, leader of a host –
  they are in the uplands of Gwanas Gwŷr.

St 28-30. Rhos Gwanas, looking towards Cadair Idris

Y beddau hir yng Ngwanas, ni chafas a'u dioes pwy wynt wy, pwy eu neges.	29 The long graves in Gwanas, whoever despoiled them did not find out who they were, what was their mission.

Teulu Oeth ac Anoeth a ddyfu ynoeth
    i eu gŵr, i eu gwas;
a'u ceiso wy, cladded Gwanas.
	30 The warband of Oeth and Anoeth came there
	    to their man, to their servant –
	whoever would seek them, let him dig Gwanas.

Bedd Llwch Llawengin ar Gerddennin afon,
    pen Saeson swydd Erbin –
ni byddai drimis heb drin.
	31 The grave of Llwch Llawengin on the river Cerddennin,
	    head of the Saxons of Erbin's land –
	he would not be three months without battle.

Y beddau yn Hirfynydd – yn llwyr y'u gŵyr lluosydd: bedd Gwrien, gwrhyd enwog, a Llwyddog ap Lliwelydd.	32 The graves on Long Mountain, multitudes know them well – the grave of Gwrien, famous for bravery, and Llwyddog ap Lliwelydd.

St 32. Tumulus on Long Mountain, near Welshpool, Montgomeryshire

Piau'r bedd yn y mynydd
    a lywiasai luosydd?
  Bedd Ffyrnfael Hael ab Hywlydd.
	33 *Whose is the grave on the mountain
	    of one who ruled hosts?
	  The grave of Ffyrnfael the Generous son of Hywlydd.*

Piau'r bedd hwn? Bedd Eiddïwlch Hir
    yng ngwrthdir Pennant Twrch,
  mab Arthan, gyflafan gyfwlch.
	34 *Whose is this grave? The grave of Eiddïwlch Hir
	    in the upland of Pennant Twrch,
	  the son of Arthan, excellent in battle.*

Bedd Lleu Llaw Gyffes y dan achles môr,
    yn y bu ei gyfnes.
  Gŵr oedd hwnnw gwir i neb ni roddes.
	35 *The grave of Lleu Llaw Gyffes under the sea's shelter,
	    where his kinsman was.
	  That was a man who yielded right to no one.*

Bedd Beidog Rudd yn amgant Rhiw Lyfnaw,
    bedd Lluosgar yng Ngheri,
  ac yn Rhyd Brydw, bedd Omni.
	36 *The grave of Beidog the Red in the region of Rhiw Lyfnaw,
	    the grave of Lluosgar in Ceri,
	  and in Rhyd Brydw, the grave of Omni.*

St 36. Two unexcavated tumuli in Ceri, Montgomeryshire

Pell ei fysgi ac argudd,
gweryd Machawy a'e cudd –
hirwynion bysedd Beidog Rudd.

37 *Far off his turmoil and hidden,*
the earth of Machawy hides him –
long and white are the fingers of Beidog the Red.

St 37-38. A burial mound in the Bachawy (Machawy) valley

St 37-38. The Bachawy (Machawy) entering the Wye

Pell ei fysgi ac anaw,
gweryd Machawy arnaw –
Beidog Rudd yw hwn, mab Emyr Llydaw.

Bedd unben o Bryden yn lleudir Gwynasedd,
    yn ydd â Lliw yn Llwchwr;
    yng Nghelli Friafael bedd Gyrthmwl.

Y bedd yn Ystyfachau
y mae pawb yn ei amau –
bedd Gwrthëyrn Gwrthenau.

38 Far off his turmoil and his wealth,
the earth of Machawy over him –
Beidog the Red is this, the son of Emyr Llydaw.

39 The grave of a chieftain of Pictland in the open land of Gwynasedd,
    where the Lliw goes into the Llwchwr;
    in Celli Friafael, the grave of Gyrthmwl.

40 The grave in Ystyfachau,
everyone doubts it –
the grave of Gwrtheyrn Gwrthenau.

St 40. Bedd Gwrtheyrn was said to have been located on a slope overlooking Nant Gwrtheyrn in Llŷn

Cian a ud yn niffaith cnud draw
    odduwchben bedd alltud –
    bedd Cynddilig ap Corgnud.

Neum dwg i Elffin i brofi fy marddrin
    gysefin uwch cynran –
    bedd Rhufawn rhwyfenydd ran.

Neum dug i Elffin i brofi fy marddrin
    uwch cynran gysefin –
    bedd Rhufawn, rhy ifanc ddaeërin.

41 *A pup howls in the wilderness of a wolf pack yonder*
    over the grave of a foreigner –
    the grave of Cynddilig ap Corgnud.

42 *Elffin brought me to test my bardic skill*
    first above a leader –
    the grave of Rhufawn with the look of a prince.

43 *Elffin brought me to test my bardic skill*
    above a leader first –
    the grave of Rhufawn, too young in the earth.

St 42-43. Bedd Taliesin, above Tre Taliesin, Ceredigion

Bedd i Farch, bedd i Wythur,
bedd i Wgon Gleddyfrudd.
Anoeth byd, bedd i Arthur.

44   *A grave for March, a grave for Gwythur,*
     a grave for Gwgon Red-sword.
     Hard to find in the world—a grave for Arthur.

St 44. Bedd Arthur, a Neolithic or Bronze Age stone circle in Mynydd Preseli

Bedd Elchwith ys gwlych glaw,
Maes Meueddog i danaw –
dylÿai Cynon yno ei gwynaw.

Piau'r bedd hwn? Bedd hwn a hwn?
Gofyn i mi. Mi a'i gwn.
Bedd ef – bedd Eiddew oedd hwn
a bedd Eidal Tâl Ysgwn.

Eiddew ac Eidal, diysig alltudion,
    cenawon cylchwy drai
    megid meibon Meigen meirch mai.

45   *The grave of Elchwith, rain wets it,*
    the field of Meueddog under it –
    Cynon had a right to mourn him there.

46   *Whose is this grave? This grave and this?*
    Ask me. I know it.
    His grave – the grave of Eiddew was this,
    and the grave of Eidal of the ready brow.

47   *Eiddew and Eidal, lively foreigners,*
    whelps with pierced shields;
    the sons of Meigen rear horses of the plain.

St 47. Pistyll Rhyd-y-meinciau on the Afon Eiddew, just above Llyn Efyrnwy

Piau'r bedd hwn? Bedd Brwyno Hir –
    hydr ei wir yn ei fro.
  Parth ydd fai, ni fyddai ffo.
	48 Whose is this grave? The grave of Brwyno the Tall –
	    Strong his justice in his land.
	  Where he would be, would be no flight.

Piau'r bedd hwn? …nid
aral gwythwch wrth erfid –
tra'th laddai chwarddai wrthyd.

49 Whose is this grave? …
the ferocity of a wild boar in battle –
as he killed you, he would laugh at you.

Bedd Silidd Dywal yn Edrywy le.
    Bedd Llemenig yn Llanelwy.
  Yng Ngwernin fre, bedd Eilinwy.

50 The grave of Silidd the Fierce in Edrywy.
    The grave of Llemenig in Llanelwy.
  In the hill of Gwernin, the grave of Eilinwy.

Bedd milwr mirain, gnawd celain o'i law
    cyn bu taw i dan main,
  Llachar ap Rhun yng Nghlun Cain.

51 The grave of a handsome warrior, common a corpse
    from his hand
  before he was silent under stones –
  Llachar ap Rhun in Clun Cain.

St 50. The small island of Carregedrywy, off the Pembrokeshire coast north of Newport

Bedd Talan Talyrth yn yngyrth teircad,
    cymynad, pen pob nyrth,
    hyged, agored ei byrth.

Bedd Elsner ap Nêr yn nyfnder daear,
    diarchar, dibryder;
    pen llu fu tra fu ei amser.

Bedd gŵr gwrdd ei fâr, Llachar, llyw nifer,
    yn aber dwfr Dyar,
    yn y gwna Tafwy toniar.

52 *The grave of Talan Thrusting Brow in the strife of three armies,*
    slayer, the head of every force,
    bountiful, his gates open.

53 *The grave of Elsner ap Nêr in the depth of the earth,*
    dauntless, fearless;
    he was head of a host in his time.

54 *The grave of a man of fearless fury, Llachar, lord of a host,*
    at the mouth of the waters of the Dyar,
    where the Tafwy makes a surge.

St 54. The Dyar entering the Teifi at Llanybydder

Piau'r bedd yn y Rhydau?
Bedd Rhwyf yw hwnnw, mab Rhygenau,
gŵr a ddigonai dda ar ei arfau.

Piau'r bedd hwn? Bedd Braint
i rhwng Llyfni a'i lledmaint –
bedd gŵr gwae ei ysgeraint.

Piau'r bedd yn llethr y bryn?
Llawer nis gŵyr a'i gofyn –
bedd i Goel ap Cynfelyn.

55 *Whose is the grave at the Fords?*
That is the grave of Rhwyf, the son of Rhygenau,
a man who accomplished good with his arms.

56 *Whose is this grave? The grave of Braint*
between the Llyfni and its tributaries –
the grave of a man who was woe to his enemies.

57 *Whose is the grave on the slope of the hill?*
Many who do not know ask it –
a grave for Coel ap Cynfelyn.

St 56. Afon Llyfni entering the sea at Pontllyfni

Bedd Dehewaint ar Glewaint afon
   yng ngwrthdir Mathafarn –
     ystyffwl cedwyr cadarn.

Bedd Aron ap Dyfnwyn yn Hirwaun le –
   ni ddodai lef ar ladron;
   ni roddai gwir i'w alon.

Bedd Taflogau ap Lludd yn ei drefred draw,
   mal y mae yn ei gystudd –
   a'i clathai, caffai fudd.

58   *The grave of Dehewaint on the river Clewaint*
     in the uplands of Mathafarn –
      pillar of mighty warriors.

59   *The grave of Aron ap Dyfnwyn in Hirwaun –*
     he would not raise a cry against a thief;
     he would not yield right to his enemies.

60   *The grave of Taflogau ap Lludd in his homestead yonder,*
     as he is in his affliction –
     whoever would dig it, he would find a fortune.

St 58. Pant-y-Saer cromlech, Llanfair Mathafarn Eithaf, Anglesey

St 60. The Nant Gau just before joining the Ystwyth at Pont Dologau

Piau'r bedd ar lan Rhuddnant?
Rhun ei enw, rhadau ceugant.
Rhi oedd ef – Rhiogan a'i gwant.

Oedd ef cyfnisen i holi galanas,
    gwaywawr rhudd, grudd addien –
a chyn bwyr budd, bedd Bradwen.

61 *Whose is the grave on the bank of Rhuddnant?*
Rhun is his name, of undoubted graces.
He was a king – Rhiogan stabbed him.

62 *He was persistent in seeking retribution for murder,*
    red spears, a fine cheek, –
and though it was for fortune, a grave for Bradwen.

St 61. Nant Rhuddnant, east of Devil's Bridge, Ceredigion

Piau'r bedd pedryfal
a'i bedwar main am ei dâl?
Bedd Madog, marchog dywal.

63 *Whose is the square grave*
with its four stones at its end?
The grave of Madog, a fierce horseman.

St 63. Maen Madog, near Ystradfellte, Brecknockshire

Yn Eifionydd, Elwydd dir,
y mae bedd gŵr hydwf hir.
Lleas pawb pan ry dyngir.

64 In Eifionydd, Elwydd's land,
is the grave of a tall, well-built man.
Everyone's death comes when it is fated.

St 64. The view across Eifionydd from one of the round huts on Tre'r Ceiri

Y tri bedd yng Nghefn Celfi,
awen a'u dywod imi –
bedd Cynon, garw ei ddwyael,
bedd Cynfael, bedd Cynfeli.

Bedd Llwyd Llednais yng Nghemais dir –
    cyn boed hir twf ei ais,
  dygyrchai tarw trin o drais.

Bedd Siôn Syberw yn Hirerw fynydd
    i rwng y gweryd a'i dderw –
  chwerthinog, bradog, brydchwerw.

65   The three graves in Cefn Celfi,
the muse told them to me –
the grave of Cynon, rough his brows,
the grave of Cynfael, the grave of Cynfeli.

66   The grave of Llwyd the Gentle in the land of Cemais –
    before his breast was full grown,
  the bull of battle attacked with violence.

67   The grave of Siôn the Proud on Hirerw mountain
    between the earth and his oaken coffin –
  mocking, treacherous, a sour disposition.

St 65. The north Cefn Celfi stone

St 65. The south Cefn Celfi stone

Piau'r bedd yn y clydwr?
Tra fu ni fu eiddilwr –
bedd Ebediw ap Maelwr.

Piau'r bedd yn yr allt draw?
Gelyn i lawer ei law –
tarw trin. Trugaredd iddaw!

Y beddau yn y Morfa –
ys bychan a'u haelewy.
Y mae Sanant, syberw fun.
Y mae Rhun, rhyfel afwy.
Y mae Garwen ferch Henyn.
Y mae Lledin a Llywy.

Bedd Henyn Henben yn aelwyd Dinorben.
Bedd Airgwl yn Nyfed.
Yn Rhyd Gynan – Cyhored.

68 Whose is the grave in the shelter?
While he lived he was no weakling –
the grave of Ebediw ap Maelwr.

69 Whose is the grave on yonder slope?
His hand an enemy to many –
a bull of battle. Mercy to him!

70 The graves on the Morfa –
Few are those who mourn them.
There is Sanant, proud maid.
There is Rhun, heated in battle.
There is Garwen ferch Henyn.
There are Lledin and Llywy.

71 The grave of Henyn Henben on the hearth of Dinorben.
The grave of Airgwl in Dyfed.
At Rhyd Gynan – Cyhored.

Parc y Meirch hoard, Dinorben

St 70. Morfa Rhianedd and the Great Orme, Llandudno, viewed from Creigiau Rhiwledyn on the Little Orme

Gogyfarch pob diara,
'Piau'r feddgor yssy yma?'
Bedd Einion ap Cunedda –
cwl ym Mhrydain ei ddifa.

Piau'r bedd yn y Maes Mawr?
Balch ei law ar ei lafnawr –
bedd Beli ap Benlli Gawr.

72 *Every mournful person asks,*
'Whose is the tomb that is here?'
The grave of Einion ap Cunedda –
slaying him in Britain was a wrong.

73 *Whose is the grave at Maes Mawr?*
Proud was his hand on his blades –
the grave of Beli ap Benlli the Giant.

St 73. Foel Fenlli, above Maes Mawr

ADDITIONAL STANZAS OF THE GRAVES

II. Llyfr Coch Hergest

Llyma yma fedd difai
tringar. Ei feirdd ry seai
ei glod lle nid elai
Byll, pe'i pellach parai.

Maen a Madog a Medel,
dewrwyr, diysig froder,
Selyf, Heilin, Llawr, Lliwer.

Bedd Gwell yn y Rhiw Felen.
Bedd Sawyl yn Llangollen.
Gwercheidw Llam y Bwch Llorien.

Bedd rhudd, neus cudd tywarch.
Nis eiryd gweryd amarch. ….
Bedd Llygedwy ap Llywarch..

Maes Maoddyn – neus cudd rhew.
O ddifa da ei oddew,
ar fedd Eirinfedd eiry tew.

Tom Elwyddan – neus gwlych glaw,
Maes Maoddyn i danaw.
Dylyai Gynon yno ei gwynaw.

II. *The Red Book of Hergest*

R1 *See here the grave of a faultless one,
fond of battle. His poets would have spread
his fame where Pyll would not go,
if he had lived longer.*

R1A *Maen and Madog and Medel,
brave men, lively brothers,
Selyf, Heilin, Llawr, Lliwer.*

R2 *The grave of Gwell on Rhiw Felen.
the grave of Sawyl in Llangollen.
Llorien guards Llam y Bwch*

R3 *A bloody grave, sod covers it
… .
The grave of Llygedwy ap Llywarch.*

R4 *Maes Maoddyn – frost covers it.
After the destruction of one well nurtured,
thick snow on the grave of Eirinfedd.*

R5 *The tomb of Elwyddan – rain wets it,
Maes Maoddyn beneath it.
Cynon had a right there to mourn him.*

St R2. Bwlch Rhiw Felen, where an earlier trackway crossed over the Horseshoe Pass, north of Llangollen

III. Peniarth Llsgr 98B

Ychwaneg o Englynion y Beddau, o law
Wiliam Salsbri, medd Rosier Morys.

Y bedd yn y gorfynydd
a lywiasai luosydd –
bedd Ffyrnfael Hael ap Hywlydd.

Bedd Gwaeanwyn, gŵr gofri,
y rhwng Llifon a Llyfni.
Gŵr oedd ef gwir i neb ni roddi.

Bedd Gwydion ap Dôn ym Morfa Dinlle
    i dan fain Defeillon.
  Garannog ei geiffyl meinon.

Neud am ddiau cwm am waith fuddig
    gŵr clod, iôr waith fuddig,
  arwynol gedol Gredig.

Gwedi seirch a meirch crychrawn
a gawr a gwewyr uniawn,
am ddinon rhythych dros odreon,
pen hardd Llofan Llaw Estrawn.

Gwedi seirch a meirch melyn
a gawr a gwaywawr gwrthryn,
am ddinau rhych bych dros odreon,
pen hardd Llofan Llawygyn.

III. Peniarth MS 98B

Additional Englynion y Beddau, from the hand of William Salesbury, says Roger Morris.

P1 The grave in the highland
of one who ruled hosts –
the grave of Ffyrnfael Hael ap Hywlydd.

P2 The grave of Gwaeanwyn, a man of renown,
between the Llifon and the Llyfni.
He was a man who yielded right to no one.

P3 The grave of Gwydion ap Dôn on Morfa Dinlle
    Under the stones of Defeillon.
  Beloved his … .

P4 … .
    a man of fame, victorious lord of battle,
  fierce, bountiful Credig.

P5 After armour and curly-tailed steeds
and battle-cry and straight spears
… .
the fair head of Llofan Foreign Hand.

P6 After armour and yellow steeds
and battle-cry and opposing spears,
… .
the fair head of Llofan … Hand.

St P2. Maen Llwyd Glynllifon

St P3. Morfa Dinlle, looking north

Bedd Llofan Llaw Ddifo yn Arro Fenai.
Yn y gwna ton tolo,
bedd Dylan yn Llanfeuno.

P7 The grave of Llofan Destructive Hand on the
bank of Menai.
Where the wave makes a noise,
the grave of Dylan in Llanfeuno.

Sts P7-P8. The banks of Abermenai

Bedd Llofan Llaw Ddifo yn arai o Fenai –
    odidog a'i gwypo,
  namyn Duw a mi heno.
	P8 The grave of Llofan Destructive Hand on the… of Menai –
	    rare is one who knows it,
	  except for God and me tonight.

Bedd Panna ap Pyd yn ngorthir Arfon
    dan ei oer weryd.
  Bedd Cynon yn Rheon Rhyd.
	P9 The grave of Panna ap Pyd in the highlands of Arfon
	    under its cold earth.
	  The grave of Cynon at Rheon Ford.

Bedd Lleu Llaw Gyffes dan achles môr –
    cyn dyfod ei armes
  gŵr oedd ef gwahoddai ormes.
	P10 The grave of Lleu Llaw Gyffes under the shelter of the sea –
	    before his time came
	  he was a man who invited attack.

Pan ddyfu Benhych a'i befyl ar afon …
    oedd arfog ei ynni.
  Llas Agen ap Rhugri
  o leas Ager yn Aber Bangori.
	P11 When Benhych came with his … on the river …
	    his power was armed.
	  Agen ap Rhugri was killed
	  after the death of Ager at Aber Bangori.

Car canhwyliaith hedd hedar luoedd ei laith	P12 ….

Bedd Tydai Tad Awen yn ngwarthaf Bryn Arien.
    Yn y gwna ton tolo
  bedd Dylan yn Llanfeuno.
	P13 The grave of Tydai, Father of Inspiration, atop Bryn Arien.
	    Where the wave makes noise –
	  the grave of Dylan in Llanfeuno.

Ciglef don drom dra thywod; am fedd Disgyrnin Disgyffeddod aches trwm anghrwes pechod.	P14 I have heard a heavy wave over the sand; around the grave of Disgyrnin Disgyffeddod a heavy sea … wickedness.

Bedd Elidir Mwynfawr yng nglan mawr Meweddus,
    ffawd brydus briodawr,
    gwynnofwr, gŵr gwrdd ei gawr.
	P15 The grave of Elidir Mwynfawr on the great bank of Meweddus,
	    fair, fortunate ruler,
	    destroyer, man with a fierce battle-cry.

Y bedd yng ngorthir Nanllau,
ni ŵyr neb ei gyneddfau –
Mabon ap Mydron Glau.

P16 *The grave in the upland of Nantlle,*
no one knows his remarkable characteristics –
Mabon ap Mydron the Swift.

St P16 Evening cloud descending on the Nantlle Ridge, seen from the slopes of Moel Tryfan

Bedd anap lleian ymnewais fynydd,
    lluagor llew Emrais,
    prif ddewin, Myrddin Emrais.

Uwch law Rhyd y Garwfaen ryde
y mae bedd Rhun ab Alun Dyfe[d].

IV. Wrexham MS 1

Piau'r bedd yn y caerau
gyferbyn â Bryn Beddau?
Gwryd ap Gwryd Glau.

P17   The grave of a nun's misbegotten son on… mountain,
    host-splitting lion of Emrais,
    chief magician, Myrddin Emrys.

P18   Above Rhyd y Garwfaen …
is the grave of Rhun ab Alun Dyfed.

IV. Wrexham MS 1

W1   Whose is the grave in the forts
opposite Bryn Beddau?
Gwryd ap Gwryd the Swift.

St W1. Looking across Nant-y-Moch towards Hyddgen, with the slopes of Bryn y Beddau in the centre right

St 12 Camlan and Bwlch Oerddrws, east of Dolgellau

Notes and Commentary

1. Cerwyd and **Cywryd** are variants of the same name, though not necessarily the same person, of course. In the Triads of the Island of Britain, Gw(e)ryd Gwent (or in some manuscripts, Cywryd Caint [of Kent]) is named as the father of one of 'Arthur's Three Great Queens' (all of whom are named Gwenhwyfar), and among the 'Three Fair Maidens of the Island of Britain', we find Gwen daughter of Cywryd ap Crydon (TYP, Triads 56, 78). A poem by Gwilym Ddu o Arfon (c. 1330) recalls the memory of *Cywryd, bardd Dunawd* (Cywryd, Dunawd's poet), who Rachel Bromwich suggests would have been one of the last of the *Cynfeirdd* or early Welsh poets, but who is otherwise unknown (TYP 335). Whether any of these is intended in the present englyn is also unknown.

Caw of Prydyn (Pictland/Scotland) was a fifth-century ruler in the Old North who was particularly remembered as the father of a number of Welsh saints, including the learned Gildas, whose *De Excidio et Conquestu Britanniae (On the Ruin and Conquest of Britain)* is one of our best surviving sources for the history of post-Roman Britain. Caw is named in the story of *How Culhwch Got Olwen* as the father of nineteen sons and one daughter. The tale tells of Arthur's hunt for the mythical boar, Twrch Trwyth, and his companion boars and how Caw killed the mythical Chief Boar, Ysgithrwyn:

> *And Arthur himself went on the hunt, with Cafall, Arthur's dog, in his hand. And Caw of Prydyn took the power of a small battle-axe, and with swift fury he came toward the boar and he split his head in two halves. And Caw took the tusk.* (CT 53)

Sts 1-3 are linked not only by their opening words, but also by the pattern of three names in the third line: the first two names rhyme and the second and third alliterate, while the third carries the main rhyme.

2. A **Gwrien** is eulogized in *The Gododdin* (see the note to St 3 below).

Morien is mentioned several times in *The Gododdin*, where he is identified as Morien son of Caradog and as a standard of comparison (Jarman, *Gododdin*, lines 366, 373, 443, 528). He and his son Bradwen (see St 62) are listed in the catalogue of names in *How Culhwch Got Olwen* (CT 28).

Morial, too, is the hero of a stanza in *The Gododdin*: 'Morial, who pursues them, bears no disgrace, / with a steely blade, ready for a stream of blood' (Koch, *Gododdin*, 103; CA 656-63). The deaths of possibly a different Morial's descendants are cited in a stanza in the *Canu Heledd*, and *Canu y Meirch* (The Song of the Horses) in the *Book of Taliesin* possibly praises his warband: *Tragwres milet Moryal / katwent kenedyl da* (The great ferocity of Morial's warband, / a good kindred in battle) (EWSP 439, 490; LPBT 393). A *Moriael* is mentioned in the seventh-century elegy for Cynddylan (for whom see the note to St 15), but this might alternatively be interpreted as *Morfael* (see also Koch, *Cunedda*, pp. 290-91). Edward Lhuyd's late seventeenth-century *Parochialia* makes reference to a *Bryn Morial* (Morial's Hill) near Oswestry (127).

The deaths of Morien and Morial are also lamented together in the later 'Prophecy of Myrddin and Gwenddydd, His Sister': 'Morgenau dead, powerful Morial dead, / Morien dead, the rampart of battle; / heaviest the sorrow for [the news of] your death, Myrddin' (RoM 45).

3. The *Gwen* of the *Black Book* may represent the name *Gwên* or it may be a variant spelling of *Gwyn*. It is likely that **Gwên**, **Gwrien**, and **Gwriad** are the same three who are named together in *The Gododdin*: 'And Gwrien and Gwyn and Gwriad. / From Catraeth, from the slaughter, / From Bryn Hyddwn before they were taken, / After bright mead in the hand, / Not one of them saw his father' (Jarman, *Gododdin*, 332-36).

4. **Tydai Tad Awen** is an obscure, apparently legendary poet, not to be confused with the sixth-century Talhaearn Tad Awen mentioned in the *Historia Brittonum*. He appears as a standard of comparison in Iolo Goch's elegy for Llywelyn Goch ap Meurig Hen (c. 1390): 'Never did Tydai Father of the Muse / … make the pure poetry he made' (Johnston, *Iolo Goch: Poems*, 93). Similarly, in the later sixteenth century, Wiliam Llŷn says of Gruffudd Hiraethog, *Tydai'n ail, Tad Awen oedd* 'He was like (a second) Tydai Tad Awen' (SC 10.251). *Awen*, often translated 'muse', is a term for 'the poetic gift, genius', or more literally 'inspiration'.

Bryn Arien (or *Bryn Aren*) is a low promontory on the coast of Arfon now known as *Trwyn Maen Dylan* (= 'Dylan's Stone Point'). It is named in the Fourth Branch of *The*

Mabinogi as Gwydion brings Lleu Llaw Gyffes (Dylan's twin brother; see St 35) to his mother Aranrhod in order to trick her into arming him in spite of her promise that she would not do so.

The remarkable circumstances of the birth of **Dylan** are told and his tragic death is alluded to pointedly in the Fourth Branch of *The Mabinogi*. The king named him Dylan (Sea), or perhaps originally Dylanw (Flood), and immediately after his baptism he took to the sea and could swim as well as any fish; thereafter he was called *Dylan eil Ton* (Sea son of Wave), with a play on the name of his mother's father, the mythological *Dôn*. Dylan is then said to have died of a blow struck by his uncle Gofannon, which is described as one of the 'Three Unfortunate Blows', though no such triad has survived independently. One of the wisdom poems in the *Book of Taliesin* asks and answers, 'Why is it noisy – / the tumult of the waves against the shore? / avenging Dylan / it reaches towards us' (LPBT 242-43). Though we do not know the underlying tale, this coupling of Dylan with the sound of the sea is undoubtedly closely related to the lines in the present stanza. Similarly the short poem entitled 'Elegy for Dylan eil Ton' in the same manuscript also places to the death of Dylan on the shore:

> *The one God above, the wisest sage, the greatest that rules:*
> *what held the metal? who fashioned it as a hand-ordeal?*
> *Before him, who was [a means of] settlement, with vice-like quality?*
> *The groom watches intently – he wrought harm, a deed of violence:*
> *the striking of Dylan on the deadly shore, violence in the current.*
> *The wave of Ireland, and the wave of [the Isle of] Man, and the wave of the North,*
> *and the fourth, the wave of Britain of the splendid hosts.*
> *I entreat the Father, Lord God Father of the realm where there is no refusal,*
> *the heavenly Creator who will receive us into [His] mercy.*
> (trans. Marged Haycock, LPBT 483)

Lines 2 and 3 of this poem may contain references to Gofannon, whose name means 'the divine smith', who struck Dylan that Unfortunate Blow. Marged Haycock discusses 'extremely tentatively' the possibility that in these lines Gofannon is imagined as undergoing a trial by ordeal – holding a hot metal tool of his trade, and that *gwastrawt* 'groom, ostler' is either a derogatory term or one that expresses a smith's connection to horses (see LPBT 478-87).

At the tip of Bryn Arien is a large boulder known as *Maen Dylan*, which has taken its name from a nearby standing stone that was still to be seen leaning over and washed by the tides in the nineteenth century, but is now fallen and lost.

Llanfeuno is an alternative early name for the village of Clynnog Fawr, in which the church is dedicated to St Beuno. The geographic proximity of Bryn Arien, about a mile and a half to the north, would seem to account for the appearance of Tydai and Dylan in the same stanza.

There are two variants of this stanza in Peniarth MS 98B; see Sts P7 and P13.

5. Ceri Cleddyf Hir is otherwise unknown. **Heneglwys** (= 'old church'), now known as St Llwydian's Church, is about a mile west of Llangefni in central Anglesey. **Mynwent Gorbre** is an old name for Heneglwys; in a manuscript of 1545-1553 the poet and antiquarian Gruffudd Hiraethog notes that 'the church of saint Corbre in Anglesey is Heneglwys in the commote of Malltraeth'.

St 4 Bachwen cromlech, Llanfeuno

St 6 Roots in the sunken forest of Maes Gwyddno at Ynyslas

6. The phrase *synnwyr fan* (of lofty wisdom), translated by Jones as 'high-minded', might alternatively be understood as *synnwyr wan* 'weak-minded'. Modern versions of the legend of Cantre'r Gwaelod (the lowland or bottom hundred), also known as Maes Gwyddno (the Plain of Gwyddno), off the coast of northern Ceredigion, tell how Prince **Seithennin**, who was placed in charge of the sea defences, became drunk and failed to shut the sluices, thus letting in the sea and inundating the land. An earlier version of the tale, reflected in the poem in the *Black Book* known as *Boddi Maes Gwyddno* 'The Drowning of the Plain of Gwyddno' or simply as 'Seithennin', places the blame on a woman named Mererid, though that poem, too, ends with a version of this stanza on Seithennin's grave.

Boddi Maes Gwyddno

Seithennin, saf di allan
ac edrychwyr di faranres môr.
    Maes Gwyddno rhy does.

Boed emendigaid y forwyn
a'i hellyngodd gwydi cwyn
ffynnon fenestr môr terwyn.

Boed emendigaid y fachtaith
a'i gollyngodd gwydi gwaith
ffynnon fenestr môr diffaith.

Diaspad Fererid i ar fan caer,
    hyd ar Dduw y dodir.
    Gnawd gwydi traha tranc hir.

Diaspad Mererid i ar fan caer heddiw,
    hyd ar Dduw y dadolwch.
    Gnawd gwydi traha atregwch.

Diaspad Mererid a'm gorchwydd heno,
    ac ni'm hawdd gorllwydd.
    G. G. traha tramgwydd.

Diaspad Mererid i ar gwinau cadr
    cedol Duw a'i gorau.
    Gnawd gwydi gormot eisiau.

Diaspad Mererid a'm cymell heno
    y wrth fy ystafell.
    Gnawd gwydi traha tranc pell.

Bedd Seithenhin synnwyr fan,
rwng Caer Cenedir a glan
môr, mawrhydig a cynran.

The Drowning of the Plain of Gwyddno

Seithennin, stand outside
and may you look upon the fury of the sea.
    It has covered Maes Gwyddno.

May the maiden be accursed
who released it after the feast —
the fountain-cupbearer of the fierce sea.

May the maid be accursed
who let it flow after battle —
the fountain-cupbearer of the barren sea.

The cry of Mererid on the wall of the fort,
    to God it is made.
    Customary after arrogance – long loss.

The cry of Mererid on the wall of the fort today,
    to God she prays.
    Customary after arrogance – repentance.

The cry of Mererid angers me tonight,
    and not easily does it come to me with success.
    Customary after arrogance – a fall.

The cry of Mererid on a fine bay horse,
    generous God has wrought it.
    Customary after excess – want.

The cry of Mererid compels me tonight
    from my chamber.
    Customary after arrogance – a long death.

The grave of Seithennin of lofty wisdom,
between Caer Genedr and the shore
of the sea, a magnificent leader.

The reference to **Caer Genedr** is obscure, but Cenedr may be a variant of the name Cynedr, which occurs in *How Culhwch Got Olwen* as *Kynedr Wyllt mab Hettwn Tal Aryant* (Cynedr the Wild son of Hettwn Silver Brow) (CO, lines 344, 708-9). The legend of the flood sprang from speculation about the remains of an ancient forest still visible at low tide on Cardigan Bay between Borth and Ynyslas.

7. **Aber Gwenoli** is the mouth of the Gwenoli, where it flows into the river Prysor, just above Y Felenrhyd.

Pryderi, the son of Pwyll the ruler of Dyfed and his remarkable wife Rhiannon, is the only character who appears or is mentioned in all four branches of *The Mabinogi*. The First Branch tells how he disappeared mysteriously the night he was born and how Rhiannon was punished. After four years the child was recovered and he was then named as a reminder of his mother's worry (*pryder*). In the Fourth Branch, Pryderi is deceitfully tricked into war and is killed. As the tale says, 'He was buried in Maen Tyfiog (= Maentwrog) above Y Felenrhyd (= Rhydyfelin) and his grave is there'. A stone pillar in the Maentwrog churchyard may be intended in *The Mabinogi*, though other legends associate it with the giant Twrog, hence the name Maentwrog (Twrog's stone).

St 7 The Maentwrog standing stone

Carrog (torrent, fast flowing stream) is a fairly common river and place name. There are rivers named Carrog in Caernarfonshire (illustrated on p. 20), Ceredigion, and Montgomeryshire. Bartrum suggests the region of Llanddeiniol along the Carrog in Ceredigion (WCD 307).

Gwallog Hir is mentioned in NLW Peniarth MS 147, a manuscript in the hand of one John ap Ivan (c.1566): *Pan aeth Gwallawc hir y dir mab Don* (When Gwallog Hir went to the land of the son of Dôn [i.e., Gwynedd]) (TYP 376). Thus, it is possible that Gwallog Hir is the same figure as Gwallog ap Lleenog, a historical ruler of the Old North who is associated with Urien Rheged and to whom two poems probably by the historical Taliesin are addressed in the *Book of Taliesin* (PT XI, XII). The first of these gives a list of his battles and the second identifies him as from the Celtic kingdom of Elmet (mod. Elfed), around Leeds in south-western Yorkshire. He is also mentioned in the ninth-century *Historia Brittonum* as one of the four kings who fought against Hussa, king of Bernicia in the late sixth century (HB chap 63). In later tradition, his name is interchanged with that of Urien in versions of several triads in the *White Book of Rhydderch* and *Red Book of Hergest*: 'Three Pillars of Battle of the Island of Britain', 'Three Bull-Protectors (?) of the Island of Britain', and 'Three Battle-Leaders of the Island of Britain' (see TYP, Triads 5, 6, 25, and pp. 375-6). He is listed as well in a stanza of a dialogue poem in the *Black Book* in which the speaker (Gwyddno?) purports to have been at the sites where various heroes died (see pp. 120 below).

Gwallog ap Lleenog appears in later medieval Welsh narrative tradition, and in the *Black Book* is the following obscure, possibly facetious, poem cursing the goose that plucked out his eye (LlDC 70). Thus there must have been some additional tale about Gwallog, now lost. Though written in the same hand, the last two stanzas are probably not part of the poem itself; they are written down the right margin and may have been placed there simply because of the mention of Gwallog.

Canys coegog yssy mor eurog a hyn
    yn ymyl llys Gwallog,
  minneu byddaf goludog.

Boed emendigaid yr ŵydd
a dynnwys ei lygad yn ei ŵydd:
Gwallog ap Lleenog arglwydd.

Boed emendigaid yr ŵydd ddu
a dynnwys ei lygad o'i du:
Gwallog ap Lleenog pen llu.

Boed emendigaid yr ŵydd wen
a dynnwys ei lygad o'i ben:
Gwallog ap Lleenog unben.

Boed emendigaid yr ŵydd las
a dynnwys ei lygad yn was:
Gwallog ap Lleenog urddas.

Nid aeth neb a fai enwog
i'r gorllwrw ydd aeth Gwallog,
yn falaen i'r feiriog.

Nid aeth neb a fai edmyg
i'r gorllwrw ydd aeth Meurig,
ar gefn y wraig yn dridyblyg.

*Because the one-eyed one is as magnificent as this
    beside Gwallog's court,
  I too shall be wealthy.*

*Let the goose be cursed
that pulled out his eye in his face:
Gwallog ap Lleenog, lord.*

*Let the black goose be cursed
that pulled his eye from its socket:
Gwallog ap Lleenog, head of a host.*

*Let the white goose be cursed
that pulled his eye from his head:
Gwallog ap Lleenog, chieftain.*

*Let the blue goose be cursed
that pulled his eye as a lad:
Gwallog ap Lleenog, noble.*

*No one who would be famous would go
the way Gwallog went,
accursed into the bramble.*

*No one who would be praiseworthy would go
the way Meurig went,
on the back of a woman bent double [lit. 'threefold'].*

8. Gwalchmai (Latin: *Walwanus*) is a prominent hero of Arthur's court whose adventures are included in numerous medieval romances. Around 1125 William of Malmesbury wrote, 'At that time [1087], in a province of Wales, called Ros [Rhos], was found the sepulchre of Walwin, the noble nephew of Arthur …. He deservedly shared, with his uncle, the praise of retarding, for many years, the calamity of his falling country. The sepulchre of Arthur is nowhere to be seen, whence ancient ballads fable that he is still to come. But the tomb of the other [i.e., Walwin], as I have suggested, was found in the time of King William, on the sea-coast, fourteen feet long: there, as some relate, he was wounded by his enemies, and suffered shipwreck; others say, he was killed by his subjects at a public entertainment. The truth consequently is doubtful; though neither of these men was inferior to the reputation they have acquired' (*Chronicle*, 315). In English, Gwalchmai is known as Gawain and is the hero of the fourteenth-century poem 'Sir Gawain and the Green Knight', in which he must trade axe blows with a green giant and also answer the question, 'What do women want most?'

St 8 Castell Gwalchmai / Walwyn's Castle, Pembrokeshire. An earthwork castle built within an Iron Age hillfort; fort entrance on right

The location of **Peryddon** is a matter of some doubt as the name was apparently applied to more than one river. Geoffrey of Monmouth's twelfth-century *Historia Regum Britanniae* mentions the *fluvium Perironis*, which is rendered in early Welsh translations as *Afon Peryddon*, and an earlier reference in a charter in the early twelfth-century *Book of Llandaf* locates Aber Periron in the area of Rockfield, near Monmouth. This is a likely site for the Aber Peryddon mentioned in the tenth-century prophecy *Armes Prydain* (Livingston, *Brunanburh*, 259). Thus it may be the stream now known as Nant Gern, which joins the Monnow by St Cenedlon's Church in Rockfield, Monmouthshire. There is also some evidence that Peryddon was an alternative name for the Dyfrdwy, the Dee, especially the stretch from Overton Madog to Holt (Evans, 'Incident,' 19). Patrick Sims-Williams speculates that Peryddon might have been an early name for the stream at Sandyhaven Pill in Rhos, Pembrokeshire. This runs down into the Milford Haven estuary from Castell Gwalchmai/Walwyn's Castle, which would accord with William of Malmesbury's account of Walwin's grave by the sea cited above (AW 50).

8-11. Cynon ap Clydno Eidyn is named in *The Gododdin* as one of the warriors who fought heroically at the battle of Catraeth. The poem has nine references to someone named Cynon, one of which unambiguously names him as Clydno's son. Cynon was later drawn into Arthurian legend, and in the *Triads of the Island of Britain* he is known as one of Arthur's three counsellors and one of the island's three most ardent lovers. He plays an important, if somewhat embarrassing, role in the Arthurian tale of *Owain* or *The Countess of the Spring*. The Cynon(s) named in Sts 8 and 10 may not be Cynon ap Clydno, though by clustering these stanzas together, it would seem that the compiler of this collection identified them all as the same, and the most famous, Cynon. The grave of (another?) Cynon is also named in St 65, and Cynon's mourning for Elchwith is cited in St 45.

A long, flat, broken stone incorporated into the wall surrounding the World War I memorial in the center of **Llanbadarn Fawr** is known as *Y Garreg Fawr*, 'The Great Stone', and was formerly part of a cromlech on this site. In his *History and Antiquities of the County of Cardigan* (1810), Samuel Meyrick notes that 'an immense stone still remains in the centre of the village, but this has of late been broken by some wicked boys making a bonfire on it'.

St 9 Y Garreg Fawr, Llanbadarn Fawr

10. Rhun ap Pyd is known only from this reference. The version of this stanza in P98B (St P9 herein) contains what may be the preferable reading Panna ap Pyd, which is the Welsh form of the Anglo-Saxon name Penda son of Pybba (died 15 November 655), king of Mercia. The patronym mab Pyd also occurs in the seventh-century Marwnad Cynddylan (discussed in Koch, *Cunedda*, pp. 284-87). The corruption of Pybba to Pyd may have been influenced, perhaps intentionally, by the Welsh word pyd (danger), as suggested by Patrick Sims-Williams (see EWSP 184). While Penda was English – or more accurately, Mercian – he did have Welsh allies in his wars against the Northumbrians, which may account for his inclusion amongst revered early Welsh heroes. However, Penda was certainly not buried in Arfon, which led Bartrum to prefer Rhun for St P9 (WCD 526).

A river **Ergryd** is not known, and it may be that *ergryd* is a common noun meaning 'a trembling', from the root *cryd* 'a shivering, a trembling; fear, dread'. It is so interpreted in TJ: 'in the rippling of a river'. The variant reading in St P9 may be a corruption of that in the *Black Book* text, or something like it. According to the Venerable Bede, Penda was killed in battle against a much smaller Bernician force 'close by the River Winwaed, which at that time was swollen by heavy rains, and had flooded the surrounding country: as a result, many more were drowned while attempting to escape than perished by the sword' (HEC 180). That this tradition points towards the survival of a memory of Penda's death in St P9 or that it suggests that we should look beyond Wales for the grave of Rhun or 'Panna' are both doubtful, given the exclusively Welsh provenance for these stanzas in general. The identification of the Winwaed is uncertain, though a location in Yorkshire, perhaps near Leeds, is likely. It might be relevant that the second element of Winwaed is Old English *(ge)waed* 'ford'.

Rheon Rhyd appears, in the form *Rit Reon*, in the triumphant final stanza of *Yr Afallennau*, the 'Apple Tree Stanzas' in the *Black Book* (LlDC 28). A Nant Rheon flows north into the Usk at Penpont, west of Brecon. Might a ford have once been located where the A40 now crosses the stream? Whatever its location, the ford is the site of a prophesied battle in which Cynan and Cadwaladr will defeat the Saxons:

Afallen beren a phren ffion
a dyf i dan gel yng nghoed Celyddon.
Cyd ceiser ofer fydd herwydd ei haddon,
yny del Cadwaladr o'i gynnadl Rhyd Rheon,
Cynan yn ei erbyn ef cychwyn ar Saeson.
Cymry a orfydd. Cain bydd eu dragon.
Caffodd pawb eu teithi. Llawen fydd bri Brython.
Cenhitor cyrn elwch, cathl heddwch a hinon.
(from *The Black Book of Carmarthen*, fol. 26b)

Sweet apple tree and red-blossomed tree
that grows in hiding in Celyddon Wood.
Although it be sought, that will be vain because of
its special virtue,
until Cadwaladr comes to his meeting at Rheon Ford,
Cynan before him attacking the Saxons.
The Welsh will prevail; splendid will be their leader.
Everyone will gain their rights; glad the honour
of the Britons.
Horns of joy will be sounded, a melody of peace and
fair weather.
(RoM 24)

11. For the significance of the phrase *Piau'r bedd…?* 'Whose is the grave …?' here and elsewhere, see p. 121-22.

12. Camlan – wherever it may be – is renowned as the site of Arthur's final battle. It is mentioned in the *Annales Cambriae* (tenth century?): *Gueith Camlann in quo Arthur & Medraut corruerunt* (The battle of Camlan, in which Arthur and Medrawd fell) (Morris, *Nennius*, pp. 85, 45). In the triad of the 'Three Futile Battles of the Island of Britain' we learn that 'the third was the worst: that was Camlan, which was brought about because of a quarrel between Gwenhwyfar and her sister Gwenhwy(f)ach' (TYP, Triad 84; also Triad 53). While the weight of academic opinion is that the site of the battle – if there was an actual battle – is likely to be the Roman fort of Camboglanna on Hadrian's Wall, this location vies with others, especially along the rivers Cam in Somerset and Camel in Cornwall. Whichever it may have been, it is likely, and not surprising, that the tradition of Arthur's last battle was relocated in Wales. There are several Welsh places named Camlan (winding/curved bank or hillside), including the swift-flowing river Camlan, which runs from south of the Rhinogydd range to join the Mawddach at Ganllwyd, north of Dolgellau, and the area along a stretch of the Dyfi below Mallwyd, southeast of Dolgellau.

The unnamed son of **Osfran** is unknown elsewhere, though an Osfran is alluded to in a twelfth-century poem to St Cadfan by Llywelyn Fardd (LlH 43). The second line of this stanza could as well be connected to the third line as to the first.

Bedwyr (English: Bedivere) is one of the earliest heroes associated with Arthur. In the earliest Arthurian tale, *How Culhwch Got Olwen*, Bedwyr is described in some detail: 'Bedwyr, who never shrank from an enterprise upon which Cai was bound. It was thus with Bedwyr, that none was so handsome as he in this Island, save Arthur and Drych son of Cibddar, and this too, that though he was one-handed no three warriors drew blood in the same field faster than he. Another strange quality was his; one thrust would there be of his spear, and nine counter-thrusts' (CT 34-5). In the triad of 'Three Battle-Diademed Men of the Island of Britain', Bedwyr is a fourth who was 'diademed above the three of them' (TYP, Triad 21), and in another triad he appears in company with Arthur (TYP, Triad 26W). In later medieval tradition, after the battle of Camlan Bedivere ministers to the dying Arthur, who instructs him to throw the sword Excalibur back into the lake from which it came.

Tryfan is the name given to several peaks, the most notable being the summit just north-east of Glyder Fawr in Snowdonia, shown at St 12 above, and Moel Tryfan, Caernarfonshire, shown here.

St 12 The summit of Moel Tryfan

13. Owain ab Urien was a prince in the northern kingdom of Rheged in the sixth century, whom the historical poet Taliesin laments in a moving elegy:

Enaid Owain ab Urien,	The soul of Owain ab Urien,
gobwyllid Rheen o'i raid.	may the Lord consider its need.
Rheged udd ae cudd tromlas,	The lord of Rheged whom the heavy greensward covers,
nid oedd fas ei gywyddaid.	it was not shallow to praise him.
Isgell gŵr cerddglyd clodfawr.	The grave of a companion renowned in song, of great fame.
Esgyll gwawr gwaywawr llifaid,	His whetted spears were like the dawn's rays,
cany cheffir cystedlydd	for no equal will be found
i udd Llwyfenydd llathraid,	to the resplendent lord of Llwyfenydd,
medel galon, gefeilad,	reaper of enemies, captor,
eisyllud ei dad a'i daid.	with the nature of his father and his forebears.
Pan laddawdd Owain Fflamddwyn,	When Owain killed Fflanddwyn,
nid oedd fwy nogyd cysgaid.	it was no more than sleeping.
Cysgid Lloegr llydan nifer	he host of Lloegr sleep
Â lleufer yn eu llygaid,	with the light in their eyes,
a rhai ni ffoynt haeach	and those who did not retreat
a oeddyn hyach no rhaid.	were bolder than necessary.
Owain a'u cosbes yn ddrud,	Owain punished them severely,
mal cnud yn dylud defaid.	like a pack of wolves attacking sheep.
Gŵr gwiw uch ei amliw seirch	A worthy man above his many-colored arms
a roddai feirch i eirchiaid.	who gave horses to suitors.
Cyd as cronnai mal caled,	Though he hoarded like a miser,
rhy ranned rhag ei enaid.	he shared for the sake of his soul.
Enaid Owain ab Urien,	The soul of Owain ab Urien,
gobwyllid Rheen o'i raid.	may the Lord consider its need.

In later legend Owain becomes one of Arthur's most famous knights and the hero of the *Tale of the Countess of the Spring*, with early versions in French, German, Swedish, Norse, and Middle English (see Thomson, *Owein*, xxii-iv). The location of **Llanforfael** is unknown.

Just south of the town of **Abererch** in Llŷn there is a lone standing stone in the sand-dunes of Morfa Abererch, and just north of the town, near Y Ffôr/Four Crosses, is a chambered tomb. Either of these may have been the site to which Rhydderch Hael's burial was assigned as traditions about him were relocated from the Old North.

Rhydderch Hael (the Generous) was a sixth-century king of Strathclyde who figures prominently in Welsh tradition, especially as one of the Three Generous Ones of the Island of Britain. In Adamnan's *Life of St Columba*, written in the seventh century, the saint prophesies that Rhydderch 'shall never be delivered into the hands of his enemies; he will die at home on his pillow …. And the prophecy of the saint … was fully accomplished, for … he died quietly in his own house.' In Scotland there remains a tradition that the massive erratic glacial deposit known as the Clochoderick Stone in Renfrewshire marks the burial place of Rhydderch Hael or perhaps has some other connection to the king.

St 13 Cromlech, Y Ffôr / Four Crosses, Llŷn with Tre'r Ceiri behind

14. If this englyn records an alternative site for the grave of the same **Owain** as in St 13, it is worth noting that Taliesin's elegy also notes a variety of colours (explicitly of his arms) followed by his fondness for horses. However, a love for and the bestowal of horses was expected of leaders, and the location at **Llanhiledd** in Gwent suggests that another Owain may be meant.

15. Cynddylan was a chieftain of Powys in the mid seventh century whose death is lamented in *Marwnad Cynddylan*, an elegy of some seventy lines, that may indeed be contemporary (Koch, *Cunedda*, pp. 231-292). He died, according to this poem, fighting in an alliance with (*Panna*) *mab Pyd*, i.e., Penda son of Pybba, the Anglo-Saxon king of Mercia (see the note to St 10). In a line difficult of interpretation the poet asks, 'Where is he buried?' or 'Where is his grave?' (see EWSP 174-89). Though the *hwn* (this) in the present englyn seems to imply specificity, this stanza does not answer the question from the earlier poem. Cynddylan is better known from the englynion in the *Red Book of Hergest* voiced through the persona of his sister Heledd as she mourns for him and her other brothers. The series begins with a prologue that locates Cynddylan's court in Pengwern, in the region of modern Shropshire:

> Sefwch allan, forynion, a syllwch
> Gynddylan werydre –
> Llys Bengwern neud tandde.
> Gwae ieueinc a eiddun brodre!

> *Stand outside, maidens, and see*
> *Cynddylan's land –*
> *Pengwern Court is a blazing fire.*
> *Woe to the youths who long for a mantle!*

Most affective, certainly to modern audiences, are the sixteen stanzas each beginning *Stafell Gynddylan* 'Cynddylan's chamber':

> Stafell Gynddylan ys tywyll heno
> heb dân, heb wely.
> Wylaf wers. Tawaf wedy.

> *Cynddylan's chamber is dark tonight*
> *without a fire, without a bed.*
> *I will weep a while. Then I will be silent.*

16. Lloegr is the modern Welsh term for England, but it seems to have originally referred to that general area of the West Midlands east of the Welsh border, more or less contiguous with the former Anglo-Saxon kingdom of Mercia.

Gwên ap Llywarch is one of the sons of Llywarch Hen, whom his father laments after having goaded him to battle at Rhyd Forlas. The traditions of Llywarch Hen, who outlived all twenty-four of his sons, have their roots in the sixth century, though the poetry in which these traditions are preserved is considerably later. The poem known as 'Gwên and Llywarch' recounts a somewhat testy dialogue between the two in which Gwên agrees to keep watch at the ford to spare his aged father, who then chides him for delaying. Llywarch then reminds Gwên to sound his horn if need be, and Gwên replies in suitably wry, heroic terms (EWSP 405, 469):

> Y corn a'th roddes di Urien
> â'i arwest aur am ei ên –
> chwyth ynddo o'th daw angen.

> *The horn which Urien gave you*
> *with its band of gold around its mouthpiece –*
> *blow on it if you come to have need.*

> Er ergryd angen rhag angwyr Lloegr,
> ni lygraf fy mawredd,
> ni ddihunaf rianedd.
>
> *Despite battle-horror before the warriors of England,*
> *I will not mar my greatness,*
> *I will not awaken maidens.*

One of the most moving poems in the cycle is Llywarch's lament for Gwên (EWSP 469-70), which begins

> Gwên wrth Lawen yd wylas neithwyr.
> [Er] addug ni thechas.
> Oer adrawdd ar glawdd gorlas.
>
> *Gwên stood watch by the Llawen last night.*
> *Despite the onslaught he did not retreat.*
> *Sad to relate on the green bank.*

A variant version of St 16 has been interpolated into this elegy:

> Prenial dywal gal ysgwn.
> Gorug ar Loegr lu cyngrwn
> bedd Gwên ap Llywarch Hen hwn.
>
> *A fierce warrior in spear fight, of ready boldness,*
> *he caused the English to be a crushed host.*
> *This is the grave of Gwên ap Llywarch Hen.*

The preceding englyn states, *Ar Ryd Forlas y llas Gwên* (Gwên was killed at Morlas Ford), and just south of Morlas Brook in Shropshire, tradition holds that a Bronze Age ring cairn on Selattyn Hill, northwest of Oswestry, is the site of Gwên's burial. A belvedere tower was built within the ring in 1847 to commemorate the sixth-century prince.

17-19. Meigen ap Rhun is not known from elsewhere, though later stanzas mention his sons Alun Dyfed (St 25) and Eiddew and Eidal (Sts 46, 47).

19. Lliaws Amir may be a reference to Arthur's son Amhar, who is mentioned as one of the guardians of Arthur's bed in the tale of *Geraint son of Erbin* (Ger 67); the name also occurs in the forms *Amr* and *Anir* in the *Mirabilia* or Wonders of Britain appended to the ninth-century *Historia Brittonum* attributed to Nennius:

> There is another wonder in the country called Ergyng. There is a tomb there by a spring, called Llygad Amr; the name of the man who is buried in the tomb was Amr. He was a son of the warrior Arthur, and he killed him there and buried him. Men come to measure the tomb, and it is sometimes six feet long, sometimes nine, sometimes twelve, sometimes fifteen. At whatever measure you measure it on one occasion, you never find it again of the same measure, and I have tried it myself. (Morris, *Nennius*, ch. 73)

Llygad Amr (the eye of the Amr; Gamber Head) is the source of the river Gamber, near Hereford. Unfortunately, we do not know whether Meigen ap Rhun might have played a role in Amir's host, or whether the reference to Amir is purely to establish the location.

20. Pant-gwyn is a region in southern Ceredigion, east of the town of Aberteifi/Cardigan in the former commote of Iscoed. The significance of **Gwynionog** is unclear. The next commote to the east of Iscoed was Gwynionydd, which name appears to bear some relation to *Gwynionog*. About a half mile south-east of the present Pantgwyn Farm on Allt Pencraig hill are two round barrows, now considerably ploughed down, which might fit the bill for the present stanza. An alternative – and much more striking – possible site for these graves is Foel Drygarn (or Moel Trigarn) in Mynydd Preseli, an impressive Iron Age hillfort with three very prominent Bronze Age or Iron Age cairns on the summit. Drawing on information obtained from Sir John Rhys, Sabine Baring Gould, in his description of the fort in 1900, notes, 'At Maesgwyn Meillionog (the white clover field) under Trigarn, is Lle Claddwyd Mon, Maelen a Madog, the burial place of the three kings Mon, Maelen and Madog… The farm on which are the graves of the three kings is occupied by Mr. Stephen Puton, who imperfectly opened one some time ago, but observed in it only some charcoal' (Baring Gould, 'Exploration', pp. 210-11). The similarity of these names to those in St 20 is highly striking, though the modern influence of the englyn itself on this tradition cannot be ruled out.

Môr and **Meilyr** and **Madog** are mentioned individually in the following three stanzas.

21. No **Gwyn** is known as a son of **Urien**, thus *ŵyr* is here interpreted as 'descendant', rather than more specifically as 'grandson'.

Gwynllŵg was a cantref in southeast Wales, between the Rhymni and the Usk. The MS reading *Gwynllywg* preserves an early spelling reflecting the name of Gwynllyw, the father of St Cadog, after whom the territory was called *Gwynllywiog*. The name survives in that of Wentloog, the coastal area between Cardiff and Newport. (A *cantref* [lit. '100 homesteads'] was an administrative district somewhat analogous to the early English 'hundred'.)

22. Môr is known only from this stanza, as is his father, at least under the name **Peredur Penweddig**. According to Gruffudd Hiraethog, Peredur Beiswyn (white tunic) was a lord of Ceredigion (also known as Peredur Beiswyrdd ['green tunic'], unless that is his brother), who built a court in Aberceiro, near Llanfihangel Genau'r Glyn (Llandre) in **Penweddig**, the northernmost cantref in Ceredigion

(WCD 539). There is no evidence for identifying him with the Arthurian hero Peredur ab Efrog.

23. Meilyr Malwynog and his father **Brwyn** are known only from this stanza. Meilyr's epithet, *malwynog* (evil, accursed), is not known elsewhere; it is derived from Latin *malignus* 'ill-disposed, wicked', which accounts for the characterisation of Meilyr in the second half of the first line. Alternatively, *Molwynog* (full, complete; luxuriant) is also known as an epithet, but the second half of the line would seem to favour the manuscript reading.

24. The place name **Rhyd Faen-ced** (the ford of the tribute stone) has not survived elsewhere, and the corrupt variant of this stanza in P18 gives a different form, *Rhyd y Garw Faen* (the ford of the rough stone). A passage in a manuscript by Gruffudd Hiraethog, now illegible but copied into another manuscript by Simwnt Fychan (c.1530-1606) reads, *Run ap Alun Dyved yr hwnn a gladdwyd yn ymyl y Ryd Galed yn y Gwynvynydd yMhenllyn. Ac yno y llas ef pann gilodd o Giltalgarth* (WCD 561-62) (Rhun ab Alun Dyfed, who was buried beside Rhydgaled (the hard/difficult ford) in the Gwynfynydd in Penllyn. And there he was killed when he retreated from Ciltalgarth). In addition, **Rhun ab Alun Dyfed** appears in some genealogies as an ancestor of Rhun ap Dinawal, a tribal patriarch in Cyfeiliog. Thus, Rhun's connections seem to be primarily in the north.

25. As his epithet suggests, **Alun Dyfed** was a legendary hero of south-west Wales, though he seems to have been remembered mostly for his sons. In addition to Rhun (in St 24), Dyfyr ab Alun Dyfed appears in the catalogues of names in the tales of *Geraint* and *The Dream of Rhonabwy*, while in *How Culhwch Got Olwen* an unnamed *mab Alun Dyfed* (son of Alun Dyfed) is named twice (TA 110; CT 111, 28, 43). The relationship of Alun's name to the village of Penalun (Penally), near Tenby, in Dyfed, or to any of the rivers named Alun or Alyn (in Denbigh, Glamorgan, and Pembroke) is perhaps more likely to be a distant etymological one than a direct connection. If Alun's father **Meigen** is the Meigen ap Rhun of Sts 17-19, that would suggest a particular interest in, or source of information about three generations of the same family – perhaps extended to four if Llachar ap Rhun (St 51) also belongs to another generation in this line.

26. Llia Gwyddel (the Irishman) is otherwise unknown. There is a massive Bronze Age standing stone known as *Maen Llia* (Llia's stone) in the Brecon Beacons, near the Afon Llia and below the summit of Fan Llia. These are a long way from the ancient tribal territory and later commote of **Arudwy**, which stretched from the Ffestiniog valley to Harlech on the coast and south to the Mawddach estuary. The rugged remoteness of Arudwy are replete with standing stones, cairns, and the like.

The name **Epynt**, as Thomas Jones points out, is derived from the place name, Epynt, which means 'horse track' or 'horse path' (TJ 109). The Gefel or Gefail is a stream that runs off the Mynydd Epynt range from Blaengefail to Abergefail into the Dulas about a mile and a half south of Llanwrtyd Wells.

27. The death of **Dywel ab Erbin**, probably in battle against Maelgwn Gwynedd, is mentioned in the very first poem in the *Black Book*, 'The Conversation of Myrddin and Taliesin', composed probably during the eleventh century: 'They killed Dywel in his last battle, / the son of Erbin, and his folk' (RoM 18). In his extensive catalogue of names, the author of *How Culhwch Got Olwen* lists three sons of Erbin: 'Geraint son of Erbin and Ermid son of Erbin and Dywel son of Erbin', as if they were brothers (CT 29; CO 219). However, A. O. H. Jarman has argued that whereas Geraint ab Erbin ap Custennin was a hero of Devon (and became an Arthurian hero with his own tale), Dywel was from Dyfed and possibly the son of Erbin ab Aircol Lawhir, a ruler of Dyfed (YMT 18, 32-3). Nothing else is known of Ermid.

Caeo is the name of a commote in Ystrad Tywi (Carmarthenshire).

28. Gwrgi (man hound) is a name well-attested from various early sources, including a seventh-to-ninth-century stone inscribed +GURCI, found in the church at Llangors, Breconshire, and four or more examples of *Gurci* are to be found amongst the copies of charters in the twelfth-century *Book of Llandaf*. However, this stanza clearly references a man from the north and a likely candidate is perhaps Gwrgi ab Eliffer Gosgorddfawr. Gwrgi and his brother Peredur figure in several triads (TYP, Triads 30, 44, 46, 70), including the 'Three Faithless Warbands of the Island of Britain', amongst whom we find 'the War-Band of Gwrgi and Peredur, who abandoned their lord at Caer Greu, when they had an appointment to fight the next day with Eda Great-Knee; and there they were both slain' (TYP, Triad 30). On a more historical note, the *Annales Cambriae* note for the year 573:

> *Bellum Armterit inter filios Elifer et Guendoleu filium Keidiau; in quo bello Guendoleu cecidit. Merlinus insanus effectus est.*

> 'The battle of Arfderydd between the sons of Eliffer and Gwenddolau son of Ceidio, in which battle Gwenddolau fell. Myrddin went mad.'

And for the year 580:

> *Guurci et Peretur filii Elifer moritur*
> 'Gwrgi and Peredur, sons of Eliffer, died.'
>   (HB 85-86)

On the other hand, Gwrgi and Peredur are inseparable in the references to them; thus Eliffer's son might not be the Gwrgi of this stanza. The reference to him as *Gwyndodydd*, 'a Venedotian, a man of Gwynedd', might also argue for a different Gwrgi, though that remains uncertain if we have here another example of the transference of early northern traditions onto the Welsh landscape.

Llawr appears twice elsewhere as the name of one of the sons of Llywarch Hen, first in a list with three other names (EWSP 472). Rowland, however, queries whether the second of these instances might not be a 'ghost name' generated through understanding the lines *Nym dygret na hun na hoen / gwedy lleas llawr a gwen* as 'Neither sleep nor happiness comes to me / since the killing of Llawr and Gwên', rather than as '… / after the death of a champion, oh Gwên' (EWSP 547). A Llawr ab Erw is listed in the catalogue of names in *How Culhwch Got Olwen*, and Triad 15 'Three Roving Fleets of the Island of Britain' (or perhaps 'Three Attacking Fleets') first names the fleet of Llawr mab Eiryf. Bromwich suggests the possibility that this might be a facetious name (Solitary son of Number) analogous to others such as *Nerth ap Cadarn* (Strength son of Strong) in the catalogue in *Culhwch*, and also that the unusual name forms in Triad 15 might be corruptions of Irish names (TYP 419). On the other hand, Llawr is attested perhaps more reliably as an actual name three times in the *Book of Llandaf* (Davies, *Llandaff Charters*, 177). In an early sixteenth-century genealogical tract *Llawr ap Llawfrodedd Farfog* appears in a tenth-century context. The semantic development of *llawr* grew out of the adjectival sense 'solitary; pre-eminent' to the nominal 'a solitary one, especially a single warrior in the forefront of battle', hence 'champion', then becoming the proper name *Llawr*.

28-30. Gwanas is mountainous tract about four miles east of Dolgellau, near Cadair Idris. In this area are the remains of a small Roman fort or marching camp, while about 200 yards south of this camp, on the edge of a field along the Nant Fridd-fawr, a tributary of the Clywedog, is an isolated boulder (no longer in its original position), with a well-defined circular cup mark of prehistoric provenance. No other early burial or funerary sites in the immediate vicinity are known. On the form *Gwanas Gwŷr*, see the Textual Note 28c below.

30. St 30 implies that there was some tale or tradition about the destruction of an entire warband. The second line is difficult to interpret, but it may be somewhat equivalent to the English idiom 'to a man', implying every last one of them. The warband of **Oeth ac Anoeth** has possible, albeit obscure and intriguing, Arthurian connections. Triad 52 enumerates the 'Three Exalted Prisoners of the Island of Britain':

> *Llŷr Half-Speech, who was imprisoned by Euroswydd, and the second, Mabon son of Modron, and third, Gweir son of Geirioed. And one (Prisoner), who was more exalted than the three of them, was three nights in prison in Caer Oeth and Anoeth, and three nights imprisoned by Gwen Pendragon, and three nights in an enchanted prison under the Stone of Echymeint. This Exalted Prisoner was Arthur. And it was the same lad who released him from each of these three prisons – Goreu, son of Custennin, his cousin'.* (TYP, Triad 52)

In *How Culhwch Got Olwen*, Glewlwyd Mighty-Grasp, Arthur's porter, in announcing the arrival at court of the young Culhwch, boasts first of his wide travels and experience, concluding:

St 29 The Gwanas Stone and a closeup of the cupmark on the bottom edge, centre

'I was once in Caer Oeth and Anoeth and in Caer Nefenhir Naw Nant. Fair kingly men I saw there. I have never in my life seen a man as handsome as the one who is at the door of the gate at this hour'
(CT 26).

The phrase *Oeth and Anoeth* in these instances and in St 30 might have been perceived as a place name, though it might easily have been thought of as personal names. The word *oeth* is a poetic word meaning 'something hard to obtain or achieve, a difficulty, or a wonder'; adjectively it has the sense 'strange, wonderful'. *Anoeth*, also restricted to poetry with the exception of the prose tale of *Culhwch*, consists of *oeth* plus the intensifying prefix *an-*, thus it has the same range of meanings as *oeth*, only more so (see pp. 114-15 and the note to St 44). The plural *anoethau* is the term used repeatedly in Culhwch for the seemingly impossible tasks that must be accomplished before Culhwch can marry Olwen.

31. Llwch Llawengin is to be compared with Llwch Llawynnawg, 'Llwch of the Striking Hand' in the poem *Pa Wr yw'r Porthor?* in the *Black Book* (LlDC 66), and with Llofan Llawyngyn 'Llofan … Hand' (Sts P5-P8).

Though no other instance of a river **Cerddennin** is known, it is indeed an apt river name: 'wandering, wanderer'. There is, however, a river Tarddennin, which is named in the 'Prophecy of Myrddin and Gwenddydd, his Sister' in the *Red Book of Hergest* (RoM 42). One wonders whether the Cerddennin might not have sprung from scribal error somewhere along the line.

Erbin's land is Devon; see the note to St 27.

32. There are three mountains named **Hirfynydd** (long mountain) which could be the site intended in this stanza. On Hirfynydd in Glamorgan, to the north of Neath, are a number of single and paired cairns and round barrows at Gelli-benuchel, Carn Cornel, and Nant-y-Cafn. There are several cairns, an extensive field of clearance cairns, and a standing stone or boundary stone at Cefn Hirfynydd Uchaf in Denbighshire. On Long Mountain, in Montgomeryshire, are several Bronze Age barrows.

The syntax leaves it unclear whether this **Gwrien** might be the brother of **Llwyddog ap Lliwelydd**; neither of them is known elsewhere. It is unlikely that Gwrien is to be identified with the Gwrien of Sts 2 and 3.

33. Is the mountain in this stanza the same as Hirfynydd in the previous stanza? With the exception of the variant in St P1, **Ffyrnfael Hael ab Hywlydd** is otherwise unknown, though the names *Fernfael* and *Farinmail* occur elsewhere (WCD 261, 264)

34. Eiddïwlch Hir (the Tall) **ab Arthan** is otherwise unknown. There is, however, a cairn, possibly Bronze Age, up the valley of the river Twrch at **Pennant Twrch**, in Montgomeryshire, which may be the intended grave site.

35. Lleu Llaw Gyffes is a main character in the Fourth Branch of *The Mabinogi*, which also recounts briefly the birth and death of his twin brother Dylan (see St 4), who had a strong affinity with the sea. Jones and Bromwich, following Lloyd-Jones, translate 35b as 'where his disgrace/shame was', which resonates nicely with the theme of shame in *The Mabinogi* (TJ 125, TYP 421, G 211). However, *cyfnes* is attested later elsewhere in the sense 'kinsman, next of kin, close relation' and on this basis the latter has perhaps the stronger claim. The kin in question would be either or both Aranrhod, his reluctant mother, or his brother Dylan. Caer Arianrhod is just offshore of Dinas Dinlle and the stone known as Maen Dylan is just over two miles down the coast. Lleu also figures several times in the legendary poems attributed to Taliesin (LPBT *Index*, s.v. *Lleu*). His origins are undoubtedly mythological; the name

Lleu is cognate with those of the Irish god Lugh Samildánach (Lugh skilled in many arts) and *Lugus*, the most widely worshipped Celtic deity, whose name survives in the cities of Lyons, Laon, Leiden, and Luguvalium (the Latin name for Carlisle in Scotland). The hillfort of Dinas Dinlle on the coast of Arfon and the nearby Nantlle valley also preserve Lleu's name, and in the surrounding countryside are numerous additional place names pertinent to his tale.

The interpretation of the last line depends on our understanding of the noun *gwir* (truth; right, that which is just, merit, legal claim). The implication is that he would give neither quarter nor praise to his enemies. Jones translates the general sense: 'a man who spared no one' (TJ 125). If we take *gwir* in the sense 'right', it may imply that he would not negotiate terms with his enemy. This might be seen as consistent with the vengeance Lleu exacts upon his wife's lover, Gronw Befr, who tried to kill him (see also the note to St P2).

36-38. Beidog Rudd appears in three consecutive stanzas, which suggests he was a figure of some significance and that there was a tale about him. However, he is known to us only here, though the name of his father, **Emyr Llydaw** (of which this is the earliest occurrence), is familiar from Geoffrey of Monmouth's *History of the Kings of Britain* as the father of Hywel (Howel, Hoelus), and he is named in later Arthurian material and in the genealogical tracts known as *Bonedd y Saint* (The Descent of the Saints). But Emyr Llydaw might not have originally been a name: *emyr* is a generic noun meaning 'emperor, king, lord', perhaps borrowed from Latin *imperium*; Llydaw is the regular Welsh name for Brittany or Armorica. *Emyr Llydaw*, therefore, literally means 'a ruler of Brittany'. Early versions of *Bonedd y Saint* name Emyr Llydaw as the grandfather of five Welsh saints, to which later versions add at least three more. In the present context it is also worth noting that there are various Breton saints and leaders with names similar to Beidog: *Budic, Bodic, Budoc*. In particular, Geoffrey of Monmouth introduces a King Budicius of Armorica who married Arthur's sister and who is later identified as the father of Hoel, king of Armorica (HRB VI.8); Welsh versions of Geoffrey's work refer to him simply as *Emyr Llydaw*. Might there be some confused memory or extrapolation that drew Emyr Llydaw into St 37 as Beidog's father? Or might Emyr Llydaw have already developed into a proper name in Welsh tradition?

In all three instances the manuscript records this name as *Beidauc Rut*. Because he regularly uses –*t*– to represent the sound of modern Welsh *dd* both between vowels and at the end of words, it is much more likely that the scribe, at least, considered the name to be the equivalent of *Beidog Rudd* (in modern spelling) than *Beiddog Rudd*.

36. Rhiw Lyfnaw may have been the name for a hill along the Machawy/Bachawy valley. **Lluosgar** is otherwise unknown.

Ceri was a commote in the district known as Rhwng Gwy a Hafren (between Wye and Severn) in the ninth and tenth centuries and later. The name survives in the village of Ceri (more fully, Llanfihangel yng Ngheri) in the modern county of Montgomeryshire.

The location of **Rhyd Brydw** is unknown. TJ modernises *rid britu* as Rhyd Bridw; AMR as Rhyd Brydw; the latter is adopted here as consistent with the conventions of the manuscript orthography. The ninth-century Pillar of Eliseg near Valle Crucis names *Britu autem filius Gwarthigirn quem benedixit Germanus quemque pererit ei Sevira filia Maximi regis* (Brydw, moreover, the son of Gwrtheyrn whom Germanus blessed and whom Severa the daughter of Maximus bore to him). His name also occurs in some pedigrees (WCD 67); Gwrtheyrn himself appears in St 40.

37-38. The **Machawy** or Bachawy (*Eng.* Bach Howey) is a stream in Radnorshire that meanders from the hills above Perthcolly around Painscastle and into the Wye near Erwood. The 'Appletree Stanzas' in the *Black Book* prophesy a two-day battle in Machawy Vale during which the English will rejoice on Wednesday and the Welsh on Thursday, and the 'Little Pig Stanzas' twice prophesy this battle as well (RoM 22, 28-29; LlDC 26, 33-34).

39. The forms *Prydain* (Britain) or *Prydyn* (Pictland, Scotland) are often confused or ambiguous in medieval Welsh texts. Here the northern location, Prydyn/Scotland, is undoubtedly meant. The manuscript reading p^rdein is emended to **Pryden**, as suggested by Thomas Jones, to provide internal rhyme with *unben* (TJ 124).

Gwynasedd is named in the poem known as *Gorchan Cynfelyn* appended to *The Gododdin* in the *Book of Aneirin* (Jarman, *Gododdin*, 68, 155), where, as here, it may be either a personal name or a place name. Here reference is to the lowland in the vicinity of the confluence of the Lliw and the Llwchwr.

The river **Lliw** flows into the **Llwchwr** estuary just below the town of Loughor (Casllwchwr), on the western edge of Swansea. The town is the site of a medieval castle within the confines of an earlier Roman military camp.

The location of **Celli Friafael** (Briafael's grove) is uncertain. If line 39b is understood to go with 39c, then we would expect a location near the Lliw and the Llwchwr (see TYP 389). In the church of St Maelog in Llandefaelog Fach, about two miles north of Brecon, there is an incised stone slab with an incised cross, the figure of man perhaps holding a club and a knife. The inscripton '+ BRIAMAIL FLOU' represents an earlier form of the name Briafael. A *Maes Briafel* in Merioneth was recorded as early as the fourteenth century, and there is a village of St Briavels in Gloucestershire on the Welsh border. The Norman castle there guarded the Forest of Dean and served as a hunting lodge for King John in the thirteenth century and as a youth hostel today.

Gyrthmwl is named as a northern leader in Triad 1, 'Three Tribal Thrones of the Island of Britain'. This may have been composed from earlier materials and prefaced to the triads in the period 1120-1150 (TYP cxi). Arthur is the Chief Prince in each of the three; the third element of the triad reads, 'Arthur as Chief Prince in Pen Rhionydd in the North, and Gerthmwl Wledig as Chief Elder, and Cyndeyrn Garthwys as Chief Bishop' (TYP, Triad 1). Triad 44 'Three Horses who carried the Three Horse-Burdens' names Heith as the 'horse of the sons of Gwerthmwl Wledig', and in Triad 63 Gyrthmwl Wledig is the third of 'Three Bull-Spectres of the Island of Britain'. In the latter, *ellyll* 'spectre' probably refers to a warrior who becomes 'outside' himself, somewhat like the Old Norse concept of the berserker. A Gyrthmwl, possibly originally a place name such as Garthmyl, is named in an englyn amongst the *Canu Heledd* (see EWSP 439, 600-1):

Bei gwraig Gyrthmwl, byddai gwan heddiw
    byddai ban ei disgyr
hi gyfa, difa ei gwŷr.

If Gyrthmwl were a woman, she would be weak today
    her cry would be loud –
she hale, her men slain.

40. The fifth-century British ruler **Gwrthëyrn Gwrthenau** (G. the Very Thin), known outside Wales more generally as Vortigern, is one of the best attested names in these stanzas. The name *Gwrtheyrn/Vortigern* derives from *gwor-* (an intensifying prefix) + *tigernos* (king). (The diaresis over the –*ë*- in the Welsh verse indicates that –*theyrn* represents two syllables.) The epithet *Gwrthenau* comes from *gwor-* + *tenau* (thin) or alternatively from *gwrth-* (against) + *genau* (mouth), i.e., 'false mouth, false speech'. Bede names him

Vertigernus in the *Chronica Maiora* (AD 725) and *Uurtigernus* in the *Historia Ecclesiastica* (AD 731). Bede may have taken the name directly from the *De Excidio Britanniae* (On the Destruction of Britain, c.540) of Gildas. There is debate, however, whether Gildas's text originally included the name which appears in some later manuscripts, but he certainly used the phrase *cum superbo tyranno* (with the proud tyrant), which could be a close, albeit sardonic, translation of the name *Gwrtheyrn* (supreme king). Drawing on Gildas, Bede tells how Vortigern invited the Saxons to Britain as mercenaries to help in his wars against the Picts and how they in turn sent for more Saxons, Angles, and Picts and began to conquer the island. The story is told in greater detail in the early ninth-century *Historia Brittonum*, which also includes other traditions about Vortigern, and his faults are summarized in Triad 51, 'Three Dishonoured Men who were in the Island of Britain':

> *And the second was Gwrtheyrn the Thin, who first gave land to the Saxons in this Island, and was the first to enter into an alliance with them. He caused the death of Custennin the Younger, son of Custennin the Blessed, by his treachery, and exiled the two brothers Emrys Wledig and Uthur Penndragon from this Island to Armorica, and deceitfully took the crown and the kingdom into his own possession. And in the end Uthur and Emrys burned Gwrtheyrn in Castell Gwerthrynion beside the Wye, in a single conflagration to avenge their brother.* (TYP, Triad 51)

The legends of Gwrtheyrn are mostly located in Wales, and the cantref of Gwrtheyrnion in western Radnorshire, may have once been the territory of either this Gwrtheyrn or another. The well-known tale of the discovery of the young boy who became the prophet-magician Myrddin (i.e., the Merlin of Arthurian legend), is set at the hill fort of Dinas Emrys. On the coast of Llŷn, below the peaks of Yr Eifl and Tre'r Ceiri, is Nant Gwrtheyrn (Gwrtheyrn's valley), in a region replete with ancient settlement and burial sites. Traditions from the eighteenth century tell of a mound near the bottom of the valley, known as 'Bedd Gwrtheyrn'. The name **Ystyfachau**, unfortunately, no longer survives as a known place name, though August Hunt has constructed a rather elaborate argument, dependent on various scribal and other errors, proposing its location at Stanage, in Radnorshire (Hunt, 'Vortigern').

41. Cynddilig ap Corgnud is otherwise unknown. Though he is called an *alltud* 'foreigner, alien, exile', Cynddilig is a native Welsh name. In medieval Welsh law the designation *alltud* generally means someone from outside Wales altogether, rather than a Welshman from a different kingdom or country within Wales (Jenkins, *Law*, 311). That wolves would howl over Cynddilig's grave is not surprising; the second element of his father's name, *cnud*, means 'a pack of wolves, dogs, or other ravenous animals'. Do we perhaps have here a metaphoric reflection of a father's lament at the death of his son, expressed sympathetically by his token animals?

42-43. The introduction of **Elffin** and the first person speaker gives us some context for understanding the supposed setting for the *Stanzas of the Graves* as a poem. These are the only characters amongst these stanzas who are not dead (with the possible exception of Arthur!). Elffin is well known from the story of Taliesin, the legendary prophet-poet, which provides a narrative to account for the earlier prophetic, legendary, and mystical poetry attributed to Taliesin, such as that preserved in the fourteenth-century *Book of Taliesin*. The first-person speaker of these two stanzas, therefore, is undoubtedly to be understood as Taliesin. Elphin had discovered the reborn infant, Moses-like, in a basket or coracle on the river Dyfi and named him Taliesin (beautiful brow). The child could already speak in

The Dyfi estuary at moonrise

verse and he brought great good fortune to Elffin. When the boy was grown, Elffin was imprisoned by Maelgwn Gwynedd for claiming that he had 'a bard who is more proficient than all the king's bards'. Taliesin came to the king's court and reduced his poets to incoherence. The tale is known only from the sixteenth century, though it is undoubtedly earlier in general outline, if not in detail (see especially Ford, *Ystoria Taliesin*; Ford, *Mabinogi*). It was humorously retold in English by Thomas Love Peacock as *The Misfortunes of Elphin* (1829). For the importance of a bard's ability to identify the occupants of graves, see pp. 121-22.

Rhufawn is a fairly common name in early Welsh tradition. The most likely figure of that name in these stanzas is Rhufawn Befr ap Dorath (or Deorthach or Dewrarth) Wledig. He is named in the list of Arthur's heroes in *How Culhwch Got Olwen*, and in *The Dream of Rhonabwy* he is one of three described as 'the best men … and the bravest, and who most hate for Arthur to suffer in anything' (CT 111). In the triads, he is one of the 'Three Fair Princes of the Island of Britain', one of the 'Three Golden Corpses of the Island of Britain', and a variant name among the 'Three Arrogant Men of the Island of Britain' (TYP, Triads 3, 61, 23). A poem in praise of Gwynedd by the poet-prince Hywel ab Owain Gwynedd opens with a couplet that is strikingly reminiscent of, though more elaborate than, the language of the *Stanzas of the Graves*:

Ton wen orewyn a orwlych bedd,
Gwyddfa Rhufawn Befr, ben tëyrnedd.

*The foamy white wave wets a grave,
the mound of Rhufawn Befr, chief of rulers.*

The location of this grave is not given, but an early fourteenth-century poem in the *Red Book* to the poet Trahaearn Brydydd Mawr mentions the grave of Rhu[f]awn as being *hyt Gawrnwy*, i.e., 'as far as/near Cawrnwy', which is probably Cornwy, along the northwestern shore of Anglesey (ETG 161-62). The fifteenth- or sixteenth-century humorous tract known as *Araith Iolo Goch* begins, *Cyfoeth Ruawn Befr vab Drothach Wledig oedd Wynedd gynt* 'Gwynedd was formerly the realm of Rhuawn Befr ap Drothach [sic] Wledig'. This corroborates a Gwynedd provenance for the tradition of Rhufawn (AP 12).

The descriptive phrase *rhwyfenydd ran* is translated 'with the look of a prince', taking *ran* as the soft mutation of *gran* (cheek, face), hence 'look, countenance'; but *ran* might also be from *rhan* ('part, portion, share'), giving 'of princely portion' (see TJ 127).

44. March is the King Mark of the romances of Tristan and Isolde. In Welsh genealogical tradition he is known as March ap Meirchion and a cousin to Arthur. Some elements and details of the Welsh tradition are independent of the French literary versions of the tale, as in the triad of the 'Three Powerful Swineherds of the Island of Britain' (TYP, Triad 26):

Drystan son of Tallwch, who guarded the swine of March son of Meirchiawn, while the swineherd went to ask Essyllt to come to a meeting with him. And Arthur was seeking (to obtain) one pig from among them, either by deceit or by force, but he did not get it.

March is also named as one of the 'Three Seafarers of the Island of Britain' (TYP, Triad 14). A folktale about March having the ears of a horse, similar to the widespread classical tale of King Midas' ass's ears, undoubtedly stems from the fact that *march* (pl. *meirch*) is a Welsh word for 'horse'; the names *March* and *Meirchion* actually derive from the Latin names *Marcus* and *Marcianus*. There is a Castellmarch near Abersoch in Llŷn.

Gwythur is undoubtedly to be identified with Gwythur ap Greidiawl, who appears elsewhere in Arthurian contexts. His name is twice found rhyming with Arthur's in the *Book of Taliesin* in 'The Song of the Horses': *a march Gwythur, / a march Gwa[w]rdur, / a march Arthur* (and Gwythur's horse, / and Gwawrddur's horse, / and Arthur's horse); and again in the 'Elegy of Uther Pendragon': 'I was used to blood[shed] around Gwythur, / ... Arthur has a [mere] ninth part of my valour' (LPBT 391, 505). The speaker of the latter poem (which is not a formal elegy) is either Uther himself or Taliesin.

Gwythur's mythic rivalry with Gwyn ap Nudd for the favours of Creiddylad, daughter of Lludd Silver Hand, is recounted in *How Culhwch Got Olwen*, in which finally Arthur

made peace between Gwyn son of Nudd and Gwythyr son of Greidawl. This is the peace that was made – to leave the maiden in her father's house, untouched on either side, and from that day on, a fight every May Day forever until Judgement Day between Gwyn and Gwythyr, and the one of them who prevails on Judgement Day, let him take the maiden. (CT 53)

It was Gwythur, too, who was instrumental in accomplishing one of the *anoethau*, the impossible tasks for which Culhwch sought Arthur's aid:

And as Gwythyr son of Greidawl one day was travelling over a mountain, he could hear a wailing and a bitter groaning, and it was a dreadful sound to hear. He rushed toward there, and as he came there he drew his sword and struck the anthill down to the ground, and thus saved them from the fire.

And they said to him, 'Take God's blessing and ours with you, and that which no man can ever accomplish, we will come and accomplish it for you.'

They are the ones who came after that with the nine hestors of flax seed Ysbaddaden Chief Giant named to Culhwch, in full measure, with none of them missing except a single flax seed – and the lame ant brought that before night. (CT 49)

In the triads Gwythur is listed as the father of one of the three wives of Arthur, all named Gwenhwyfar (TYP, Triad 56; see also the note to St 1 above).

Gwgon Gleddyfrudd also has tentative Arthurian connections, though he also appears independently of Arthur, and indeed he moves through time rather freely. The evidence of genealogical tracts connect him with Ceredigion at a later period, and Rachel Bromwich raises the possibility that he may be the *Guoc(c)aun rex Cereticiaun* whom the *Annales Cambriae* list as having drowned in 871 (HB 48, 89). He appears in the triads as one of the 'Three Gate-Keepers at the Action of Bangor Orchard', which might be a term for the battle of Chester in 616 (TYP, Triad 60). *In The Dream of Rhonabwy* Gwgon is named as one of three companions of Owain ab Urien 'who were sorry that loss should come to Owain' during the latter's contest of wills and *gwyddbwyll* (a board game) with Arthur (CT 111).

Arthur, one of the most popular characters in western literature for 800 years and more, hardly needs an introduction. The importance of the present stanza is that it provides important early evidence for the development of the belief that Arthur did not die, as discussed more fully on pp. 114-15 (see also the note to St 8).

45. A variant of this stanza is printed as St R5 herein. For the variant **Elchwith/Elwyddan**, see the note to St 64. **Meueddog** is otherwise unknown, but is not dissimilar to *Maoddyn* in Sts R4 and R5.

Rowland speculates that the identification of **Cynon** in St R5 as Cynan ap Cyndrwyn, a brother of Heledd, may have attracted the two 'stray' *beddau* Sts R4 and R5 into the Heledd material in the *Red Book*. The pairing of the names of Cynon and Elchwith/Elwyddan here, coupled with that of Elwydd in St 64 followed by Cynon in St 65, seems to suggest a tale of a relationship between them that is now lost. The third line is long, and perhaps *yno* (there) should be omitted, as it is in R5.

46-47. It is noteworthy that **Eiddew** and **Eidal** are mentioned together in these two stanzas, for they also appear in place names in relatively close geographic proximity. For example, to the east of Penmachno, along the river Eidda, which flows into the Conwy, are a number of place names containing the element Eidda (a derivative form of Eiddew), and in Cwm Penmachno is a farm known as Bryn Eidal. There is a Bronze Age cairn on the summit of Moel Eiddew, east of the Dyfi above Machynlleth, while there is a Pant Eidal closer to the Dyfi estuary. The river Eiddew flows southeast into Llyn Efyrnwy, and a pair of cairns and a hut circle and enclosure lie to the west of Llyn Eiddew Bach in Merionethshire. Nothing further is known of **Meigen**, except that another son, Alun Dyfed, appears in Sts 24 and 25.

48. Brwyno Hir (the Tall) is known only from this stanza and in the Ceredigion landscape. The Brwyno stones, forming a rare stone alignment for the area, have recently been located in a reforested tract near the Afon Brwyno northeast of Brwyno Farm, above Eglwysfach in northern Ceredigion. A few miles to the south is the village of Cwmbrwyno between Goginan and Ponterwyd.

St 48 The Brwyno Stones above Glandyfi, overlooking the Dyfi valley

49. The first line of this stanza is corrupt. Assuming that *nid* is the correct rhyming syllable, it would seem that at least two syllables have been lost between *hun* and *nid*. It is also difficult to determine whether *nid* represents the negative particle, which would make the syntax unclear, or perhaps the last syllable of a lost name or other phrase. In the second line, the manuscript *ervid* can be understood as either *erfid* (blow, thrust; battle, fight) or *erwyd* (spear) (see TJ 126).

50. Silidd Dywal is not known elsewhere. The name **Edrywy** appears in *Traeth Edrywy* (Edrywy strand or beach), the Welsh name for Newport Sands in Pembrokeshire. Just to the north is *Carregedrywy* (the rock of Edrywy), about 200 yards offshore from Pen y Bâl.

The shadowy figure of **Llemenig** is mentioned in several sources in contexts with a connection to the sagas of ninth-century Powys. Amongst the *Canu Heledd* are two englynion suggesting, but not clarifying, a tale about him:

St 50 Traeth Edrywy, with Carn Ingli hillfort on the horizon

[Celyn] a sych o du tan
pan glywyf godwrf godaran
llu Llemenig mab [Mawan].

Arbennig lleithig llurig ynghyhoedd
aergi gwyth gwaithfuddig
fflam daffar llachar Llemenig.

Holly dries beside a fire.
When I hear noisy tumult
it is the host of Llemenig mab Mawan.

Lord entitled to sit on the dais, openly armed,
ferocious, victorious hound of war,
a maker of flame is ardent Llemenig.

(EWSP 445, 494)

Llemenig's name is coupled with that of Heledd and Llywarch Hen in Triads 65 and 77, 'Three Unrestricted Guests of Arthur's Court, and Three Wanderers: Llywarch the Old, and Llemenig, and Heledd'. The same names appear in Triad 76 'Three Violent(?) Ones of the Island of Britain', probably by mistake. In the 'Song of the Horses' in the *Book of Taliesin* is a couplet that may name Llemenig's horse: '*Yscwydurith' yscodic / gorwyd Llemenig*, which may be translated as 'skittish "Dappled Withers" / Llemenig's steed', though Haycock translates *llemenig* as an adjective, 'a bounding steed' (LPBT 392, 400). Perhaps under the influence of this latter passage, a variant of Triad 43 'Three Pack-Horses of the Island of Britain' more explicitly names *Ysgwydvrith march Llemenic mab Mawan* ' "Dappled Withers", the horse of Llemenig son of Mawan' (TYP, Triad 43).

Llanelwy, between the rivers Elwy and Clwyd, is the Welsh name for the cathedral city of St Asaph, where a monastic community was founded by Asaph in the late sixth century.

Gwernin bre signifies a hill (*bre*) of alder trees (*gwern*), but it has not survived as a specific place name in Wales. In the *Life of St David*, however, we read that David's disciple Aidan established a monastery in Ireland *quod Hibernensi lingua Guernin uocatur* 'that is called Gwernin in the Irish tongue', and which is referred to as *Dinas Guernin* in the Welsh versions of the saint's life (RLSD 16, 39).

Eilinwy is not known elsewhere.

51. Llachar ap Rhun is otherwise unknown, but see the note to St 25. The location of **Clun Cain** is unidentifiable; rather than a specific toponym, *yng nghlun cain* might be a generic phrase with the sense 'a fair meadow/moor' or 'the ridge of a meadow'. Each of these elements occurs separately in various place names. See also St 54.

52. Talan Talyrth may be the same Talan named and lamented as a son of Llywarch Hen, though Talan does not appear in the earliest list of Llywarch's sons (WCD 592-3):

Pell odyman Aber Lliw,
pellach andwy gyfedliw.
Talan, teleisty deigyr hediw.

Far from here is Aber Lliw;
further is reproach.
Talan, you deserved tears today.

(See EWSP 412, 414, 472-3)

53. Elsner ap Nêr is not known elsewhere.

54. It is hard to say whether the Llachar in this stanza is the same as or different from Llachar ap Rhun in St 51. The name means 'radiant, flashing, brilliant, bright'.

There is a river **Dyar** ('noisy', also spelled *Duar*), that flows into the Teifi above Llanybydder. However, the Teifi may not be the river **Tafwy** named in the next line. The root form **tam-*, 'black, dark', underlies numerous river names, including Taf, Tawe, Teifi, Teme, and Thames. Of these, *Tawe* is perhaps the most likely modern development from Tafwy (*Tavue* in the manuscript). Even if we accept that as the proper name, two englynion in the 'Conversation between Gwyddno Garanhir and Gwyn ap Nudd', also in the *Black Book*, actually comment on an uncertainty of identification. Gwyddno identifies himself to Gwyn and then says,

> *The white horse does not allow me conversation with you.*
> *He leads with his bridle.*
> *He hurries to my battle of Tafwy [tawuy] and Nedd.*
>
> *It is not the nearest Tafwy [y tawue nessaw] I speak to you about*
> *but the Tafwy furthest away [y tawue eithaw]*
> *by the shore of the sea, a fierce ebbing.*

(*EWSP* 506, 461)

The parallelism between the 'fierce ebbing' in this poem and the 'surge' in St 54 make it likely that the same river may be meant in each.

55. There are various places bearing the name or the name element **Rhydau** (fords), including those in the counties of Caernarfon, Merionnydd, Denbigh, Carmarthen and Pembroke.

Rhwyf ap Rhygenau is not otherwise known. As a generic noun *rhwyf* means 'king, lord, ruler'. The second line of this englyn is long, thus Jones deletes *hwnnw* (that) and translates ''Tis the grave of Rhwyf, son of Rhygenau'.

56. Braint may be the Braint Hir (B. the Tall) ap Nefydd who appears in *Brut y Brenhinedd*, the Welsh versions of Geoffrey of Monmouth's *History of the Kings of Britain*, and who corresponds to Geoffrey's Brianus/Brian in Book 12. Braint advises his uncle, Cadwallon, not to allow the Saxon Edwin to wear a crown, thus exacerbating the enmity between the Britons and the Saxons. In another episode the king, shipwrecked on the isle of Guernsey, falls ill and desires venison to eat. None being available on the island, Braint cuts off a piece of his own thigh, cooks it with herbs, and serves it to Cadwallon, who then recovers from his illness.

Three fragments, five lines in all, of a poem apparently in praise of Cadwallon survive in a seventeenth-century manuscript under the title *Gofara Braint*, though the original from which they were copied was perhaps much older. If we emend the obscure term *gofara* to *gofera* (floods), the title may refer to the flooding of the river Braint in Anglesey and may thus have no connection to the hero Braint buried near the Llyfni (Gruffydd, 'Canu Cadwallon', pp. 41-43). On the other hand, if we suspend judgement about *gofara* and recall the connection between Braint and Cadwallon, these fragments and their title may preserve an additional, though uncertain, bit of evidence for the existence of the Braint of this stanza. We should note, too, that several heroes in these stanzas bear the names of rivers (or vice versa), as Eiddew, Brwyno, Taflogau, and Cynfael (Sts 46, 48, 60, 65). Though the river name Braint derives from that of the ancient Celtic river goddess *Brigantia*, both the river and the hero's name Braint share a common etymology with the words *braint* (privilege, title, status) and *brenin* (king).

The **Llyfni**, in Arfon, reaches the sea just north of Maen Dylan (see St 4). There are several cairns suitably located among the hills between the Llyfni and its tributaries, the Afon Crychddwr and the Afon Ddu. The Llyfni is also cited in St P2.

St 56 Stepping stones over the river Braint, Anglesey

St 57 Sarn Gynfelyn

57. This reference to **Coel ap Cynfelyn** is unique. He should not be confused with various other real or fictitious figures named Coel. Nor should any of these be identified as the Old King Cole of the English nursery rhyme, who seems to derive from a sixteenth-century clothier from Reading named Cole-brook who was known as 'Old Cole' (WCD 134-36). Sarn Gynfelyn is a natural spit of shingle that extends some way into the sea north of Aberystwyth. It is often connected to the legend of Cantre'r Gwaelod (see St 6).

58. The name **Dehewaint**, though not the man of this stanza, is attested in the *Book of Llandaff* in a charter of c. 975 (Davies, *Llandaff Charters*, 125).

The river **Clewaint** is otherwise unknown, but the name **Mathafarn** is found in Anglesey, in Montgomeryshire, and in the variant form *Bathafarn* in Denbighshire. Five 'long cist', slab lined graves, perhaps part of an early medieval cemetery, were found in 1954 at the Ty'n-y-Felin stone quarry in Llanfair-Mathafarn-Eithaf, Anglesey. (Coflein, s.v. *Long cist burials encountered in Ty'n-y-Felin quarry*).

59. Aron ap Dyfnwyn is known only from this reference. The second line of the stanza does not mean that he would let a thief escape, but rather that he would deal with a thief by himself without calling for help. Hirwaun lies in the Cynon valley about four miles from Aberdare. There are two Bronze Age cairns on **Hirwaun** Common, Craig-y-bwlch and Tarren-y-bwlch.

60. Taflogau is one of several personal names in these verses that are derived from place names (see *Epynt*), rather than the other way around. Thomas Jones points out that *Taflogau* (spelt *Tawlogev* in the manuscript) is an old name for the stream named Dologau or Nant Gau that joins the Ystwyth near Hafod Uchdryd and also the old name of another, now called Logau Las, that flows into the Ystwyth near Pontrhydygroes (TJ 109-10). Pont Dologau, the late eighteenth-century bridge over the Nant Gau, was built for Thomas Johnes of Hafod as part of his estate improvements and was recorded in an early source as Tyloge Bridge.

Lludd, who is named here as Taflogau's father, is the hero of *Cyfranc Lludd a Llefelis* (The Story of Lludd and Llefelys) which was incorporated into some of the Welsh translations of Geoffrey of Monmouth's *History of the Kings of Britain* and which is found independently in the *Red Book of Hergest* and, in part, in the earlier *White Book of Rhydderch*. The tale is also referenced in a short prophetic poem in the *Book of Taliesin* as *ymarwar Llud a Llefelys* (The discourse of Lludd and Llefelys) (see CT 89-94, 122-23).

61. Rhuddnant (red stream) is probably the Nant Rhuddnant which joins the Merin to form the Mynach,

St 60 The site of the Logau Las lead and silver mine, near Ysbyty Ystwyth, Ceredigion

which then falls dramatically into the Rheidol at Devil's Bridge. While it is not directly on the bank of the Rhuddnant, there is a much ruined Bronze Age cairn above the stream on the summit of Pen y Garn.

It is not known which, if any, of various heroes named Rhun, this particular **Rhun** might be; see Sts 10, 17-19, 24, 51, 70.

No tales clarifying the death of a Rhun at the hands of **Rhiogan** are known. The latter is identified as 'son of the king of Ireland' and is listed among Arthur's counsellors in *The Dream of Rhonabwy*; his name is given as *Rhioganedd* in the catalogue of names in the tale of *Geraint* (CT 111; TA 110).

62. A **Bradwen** is named three times in T*he Gododdin*, where we are told that he was the equal of three men for the favour of a maiden and that 'From the encounter of strife and destruction / Bradwen did not escape; he died' (Jarman, *Gododdin*, 446, 454). In lines 526-28 his name is coupled with that of his father, Morien (see St 2); both 'Bradwen son of Moren Mynawg, and Moren Mynawg himself' are mentioned near the beginning of the extensive catalogue of names in *How Culhwch Got Olwen*. Later in the same list, another Bradwen is named as one of the sons of Iaen, along with Moren, Siôn (see St 67), Caradog, and two other brothers (CT 28, 29). This may be more an example of how the author of *Culhwch* expanded his list than a record of specific traditional characters; a second list of six sons and a daughter of Iaen in the *Hanesyn Hen* genealogical tract has only the names Siôn and Caradog in common with the names in the tale (WCD 376).

63. Madog is a common name in early sources and traditions, and thus without a patronymic it is not possible to identify this particular Madog (see also Sts 20-21).

Maen Madog is an impressive standing stone, almost 9 feet high, beside a stretch of Roman road just north of Ystradfellte in Brecknockshire. In spite of the name Maen Madog (Madog's stone), it bears the early medieval inscription DERVAC – FILIUS/IVST – (h)IC IACET, 'Here lies Dervac(us), son of Iust(us)'. It has been suggested that it may have been a prehistoric standing stone, later inscribed. The stone had fallen and was re-erected about 5 metres to the north in 1940. No evidence of human remains were found in the original pit, either because the acid soil had destroyed it, or because the stone was dedicated as a memorial to Dervacus, rather than as his grave marker (Coflein, s.v. *Maen Madoc*).

64. Eifionydd was a commote at the upper end of the Llŷn peninsula to the south of Arfon.

St 63 The inscription on Maen Madog

The name **Elwydd** is attested in the *Book of Llandaff* in a charter (perhaps spurious) in which Awst, king of Brycheiniog, is named with his two sons, Elwydd (in the form *Elguid*) and Rhiwallon (BLl 146). The diminutive form *Elwithan*, i.e., *Elwyddan*, also occurs in the *Red Book* variant of St 45 (see the note above), where the *Black Book* has *Elchwith*. Elwydd is an earlier form of the name Elwa, which survives in Cadair Elwa, earlier *Caderelweth* (Lloyd-Jones, *Enwau Lleoedd*, 109), near Ynys, within the former commote of **Eifionydd**. A standing stone in Arfon is also known by the name Cadair Elwa.

65. There are two standing stones still to be seen near **Cefn Celfi** farm, just east of Rhos, Pontardawe, in Glamorgan, but Thomas Jones was assured by elderly people from Rhos in the early 1930s that there used to be three (TJ 113). The two existing stones have been much damaged in modern times.

For **Cynon** and a possible relationship with Elwydd in the previous stanza, see the notes to Sts 8-11 and 45.

Cynfael is the Welsh form of earlier *Conmail*, who is recorded in the *Anglo-Saxon Chronicle* as one of three British kings who were slain by the Anglo-Saxon king Ceawlin of Wessex at the battle of Deorham (probably modern Dyrham, in Gloucestershire) in 577 (WCD 141).

Cynfeli may stem from the form *Cynfelif* or earlier *Cinbelim*. The name is otherwise unknown.

St 64 Cadair Elwa stone, Arfon

66. The identity of **Llwyd** is not known. His epithet, *llednais*, means 'courteous, well-behaved, temperate, kind(ly), gentle', etc. John Rhŷs identifies him with Llwyd ap Cil Coed, a character in the Third Branch of *The Mabinogi*, connecting Llwyd with the cantref of Cemais in northern Pembrokeshire (*Y Cymmrodor* XVIII, 1905, 135). However, as Thomas Jones points out, there is a **Cemais** 'found in almost every county in Wales'. Following Jones, lines b-c can be read 'though long was the growth of his ribs, / the bull of battle attacked him violently' (TJ 111, 131). There are also several standing stones in Wales known as Maen Llwyd, which can be translated as either 'grey stone' or 'Llwyd's stone'. The Parc Maen Llwyd stone is located in a private garden in Puncheston in Cemais.

67. For a possible identification of **Siôn**, see the note to St 62 above.

Hirerw (long-acre) is cited in several sources as an early form of *Hirael* in Bangor, Caernarvonshire. *Hir erow* is also noted by Melville Richards near Treffynnon in Flintshire in a mid-seventeenth-century source (AMR, s.v. *Hirael, Hirerw*).

68. Ebediw ap Maelwr is not otherwise known.

69. This stanza is the only one for which no name and no other context are given. Might this have been seen as a fitting, open-ended final stanza for the poet/compiler/scribe of these pages?

70-73. These stanzas were added to the manuscript at a later date than the previous ones; see p. 124.

70. This is the only stanza that contains the names of women – **Sanant, Garwen, Lledin,** and **Llywy**. While *morfa* is a very common place-name element, it is as certain as such things can be that the **Morfa** in question is *Morfa*

St 66 Parc Maen Llwyd standing stone

Rhianedd (sea-strand of the maidens), between Great Orme's Head and Little Orme's Head. There is a Neolithic chambered burial tomb (*Llety'r Filiast*), along with other prehistoric remains, at Great Orme's Head, and at Little Orme's Head are the Creigiau Rhiwledin (the rocks of Lledin's hill). This is not an englyn, but rather a six-line series in *awdl-gywydd* metre, with seven syllables in each line and lines 2, 4, and 6 rhyming.

Sanant, the daughter of Cyngen of Powys and the sister of Brochwel Ysgithrog, was the first wife of Maelgwn Gwynedd, the sixth-century king who was excoriated by Gildas in his screed *On the Ruin and Conquest of Britain*, and whose principal court was close to Morfa Rhianedd at Deganwy. Maelgwn also had a son named **Rhun**, probably by his second wife, Gwallwen ferch Afallach, if she is not, indeed, entirely a figure of fable (see WCD 438-442).

Garwen, miswritten as *earrwen* in the manuscript, was the daughter of Henyn Henben, who figures in the following stanza. Etymologically, her name means 'fair leg'. In the Triads she appears as one of Arthur's three mistresses (TYP, Triad 57).

No tales of either **Lledin** or **Llywy** are known. The name **Lledin** is preserved in that of *Rhiw Lledin* (Lledin's hill) and *Creigiau Rhiw Ledin* (the Rocks of Rhiw Lledin).

St 70 Llety'r Filiast cromlech, Great Orme's Head

Deganwy, the fortress of Maelgwn Gwynedd, overlooking the Conwy estuary

Melville Richards notes **Llywy** as a place name, in the form *Lowey*, near Cwmhir on the 1833 OS map.

71. Henyn Henben 'H. Old-head' is the father of Garwen named in the previous stanza as one of the four women buried on Morfa Rhianedd. He may be the Henben of which the 'Elegy to Uther Pendragon' in the *Book of Taliesin* states, 'It was I who gave Henben / swords of great protective power' (LPBT 506). He(i)nin Fardd is named as the chief poet of Maelgwn Gwynedd in the sixteenth- and seventeenth-century versions of the *Story of Taliesin* (Ford 1992, lines 200, 374, 380; Ford 1977, pp. 167, 171). If the compiler/poet of the *Stanzas of the Graves* knew him as Maelgwn's poet, this would help account for Henyn's appearance following a stanza with several other connections to Maelgwn.

Dinorben, a large hillfort on a promontory overlooking the lowlands of the vale of Clwyd, was occupied from the eighth or ninth century BC until the late fourth century AD. The hillfort was completely destroyed by limestone quarrying during the twentieth century, but a series of excavations carried out between 1912 and 1984 have recorded the site in considerable detail. The Iron Age Parc-y-Meirch hoard of bronze horse harness fittings now in the National Museum of Wales was discovered at Dinorben in 1868 in association with human bones, perhaps a burial. Dinorben Lodge long cairn, a low semi-circular mound bisected by a fence, is thought to be the remains of a chambered tomb. The north side is obliterated and the centre has three large stones buried under smaller stones, as it has been used as a clearance cairn over the years.

Airgwl, known as Aergwl Lawhir (A. long-hand) was a fifth- or early sixth-century king of **Dyfed**. The first poem which Ifor Williams ascribes to the historical heroic poet Taliesin is a poem in praise of Cynan Garwyn of Powys, in which the poet mentions Cynan's attack against Aergwl: *kat yg cruc dymet. aircol ar gerdet* (A battle at Crug Dyfed – Aergwl in flight) (PT 1; my translation). A passage in the *Book of Llandaff* tells how St Teilo ended a plague in Airgwl's court in which a man died every night after feasting and (over)drinking, in return for which the king gave the saint three towns (WCD 4).

It may have been the naming of Airgwl, known from Taliesin's poem to Cynan Garwyn, that made the poet think of **Rhyd Gynan** (Cynan's ford), Cyhored's burial place. Egerton Phillimore's guess that the Pembrokeshire/Dyfed place name *Canaston Bridge* derives from an earlier *Cananyston*, and that that bridge may have been built on the site of an earlier ford, possibly known as Rhyd Gynan (DP II, 348-49; WCD 162), is only correct at several removes. Canaston seems to have derived its name from one William Canan (or a forebear of his, perhaps), known to have held land in the lordship of Narberth in 1347; The name Canan may possibly be derived from earlier Welsh *Cynan*, but the placename Canaston/Cananyston is clearly an English-language construction (see PNP 2.245).

Cyhored is named in the Triads of the Horses: *Awydavc Breichir march Kyoret eil Kynan* (Eager Long Fore-Legs, horse of Cyhored son of Cynan) (TYP, Triad 39, also in the *Black Book* version of Triad 38). The Cynan from whom Cyhored is descended is probably Cynan Garwyn, whose horse is also named in Triad 39.

72. Einion ap Cunedda is listed among the eight brothers who came with their father from Manaw Gododdin in the North, i.e., Prydyn/Pictland, and invaded much of Wales, establishing kingdoms in the northern and western coastal regions in the early fifth century. The text reads **Prydein**, which Jones understands as a reference to the North, but which might also denote *Britain* (TJ 133), as translated here. Einion appears as Einion Yrth (E. the fierce, strong, mighty) in the earliest pedigrees. Peter Bartrum suggests that Einion was allotted the district of Rhos in Gwynedd (see WCD 152, 232), which includes Morfa Rhianedd and Dinorben, named in Sts 70 and 71.

73. While there are numerous instances of the name **Maes Mawr** around Wales, the most likely for the present context in connection with **Beli ap Benlli** is that to the east of the summit of Foel Fenlli, with its Bronze Age cairn. The great seventeenth-century scribe, John Jones of Gellilyfdy, copied the following incident into Peniarth MS 267 (c. 1635):

> *There is a spot on the mountain between Iâl and Ystrad Alun above Rhyd y Gyfarthfa, called Y Maes Mawr where occurred the battle between Meirion ap Tybion and Beli ap Benlli Gawr; and there Beli ap Benlli was slain. And Meirion erected two standing stones, one at each end of the grave. These were there up to the last forty years.*

Bartrum includes a further reference that the stones stood by the eponymous Nant y Meini (Brook of the Stones) (WCD 37).

St 71 Dinorben Lodge cairn, to the left

Notes to Additional Stanzas of the Graves

Red Book of Hergest

R1-R3
These stanzas are found in the *Red Book*, column 1038.35-44, among a series of englynion about the loss of the sons of Llywarch Hen, traditionally twenty-four in number, twelve of whom are named here (CLlH 7; EWSP 411-12, 472).

R1
This stanza is fairly irregular and presents several problems of reading and interpretation; see the textual notes below and EWSP 532.

R1A
While this englyn is not a 'Beddau' stanza per se, it is included here as part of this short series of grave stanzas.

R2
On **Rhiw Felen**, Rowland quotes from an eighteenth-century commonplace book of Evan Evans which cites this stanza:

> At a place called Rhiw felen, which lies near the road leading from Llan Egryn to Dolgelley, within a mile and a half of Llwyn Gwrai, is shown the grave of Gwell, one of the sons of Llywarch Hen. That it is really so, appears beyond a doubt from the following lines handed down to posterity by the father of the person here buried
>
> vis Bedd Gwell yn y Rhiw Felen
>   Bedd Sawyl yn Llann Gollen
>   gwercheidw Llafur Bwlch Llorien.
>
> *The grave consists of two stones placed side ways at the distance of 14 inches.*
>
> *Mr. Rd. Thomas took a sketch of the grave of Gwell, one of the 24 sons of Llywarch Hen (who all perished in their father's battles) as it appears this day in a place called Rhiw felen in the parish of Llann Egryn.* (NLW MS 2029; EWSP 71)

Ifor Williams, however, posits that another Rhiwfelen about five miles north of Llangollen might be a more likely location, given the mention of Llangollen in the next line (CLlH 93). While the location of **Llam y Bwch** ('buck's leap') is unknown, Williams suggests that it would be a natural enough name for a mountain pass (CLlH 93).

R3
The second line of this stanza remains obscure, the chief difficulty being the meaning of *eiryd*, along with uncertainty as to whether *ammarch* might represent *amarch* (disgrace, dishonour; oppression) or a place name. William Owen Pugh in 1792 noted, 'There is a *Dôl Ammarch in Montgomeryshire*' (CLlH 94); compare *gweryd Machawy* (the earth of Machawy) in St 37.

Llygedwy ap Llywarch appears as *Llynghedwy* in the 'Hanesyn Hen' tract (WCD 421), and Ifor Williams notes that there is a Bryn Llyngedwy near Four Crosses, Pwllheli (CLlH 94).

R4-R5
These stanzas are found in the *Red Book*, column 1048.37-40, among the poems of Heledd (CLlH 47; EWSP 443, 493; see p. 125).

R4

Maes Maoddyn, like *Maes Meueddog*, the form appearing in St 45, is otherwise unknown. **Eirinfedd** is also unknown; Rowland points out that the name plays on the words *eiry* (snow) and *bedd* (grave) (EWSP 610).

R5

See the notes to St 45, of which this is a variant.

Peniarth MS 98B

NLW Peniarth MS 98B is in large part a copy of the *Black Book of Carmarthen*. Immediately following this copy is a group of additional stanzas with the heading as given.

P1

This is a variant of St 33, which is in the form of questioning stanza, *Piau'r bedd …?* 'Whose is the grave …?' This is a fairly clear example how largely formulaic englynion may be altered through oral transmission.

P2

Gwaeanwyn (emended from the MS *y Gwanwyn*) is better taken as a personal name than as the generic noun for 'Spring', of which *gwaeanwyn* is an earlier form. The **Llifon** enters the sea about a mile north of the **Llyfni**. The third line of the stanza is a close variant of that in St 35. This suggests that it is a stock line meaning simply that he would never yield his right to anyone, but it is worth noting that St 35 praises Lleu Llaw Gyffes, much of whose tale is also located in the vicinity of the Llyfni; see the note to St 35. The massive Maen Llwyd Glynllifon, just over ten feet high, is one of only two standing stones between the Llifon and the Llyfni. It is also one of the few Welsh standing stones to have been excavated. In 1875 fragments of a later Bronze Age urn with cremated bones and charcoal were found associated with it, a rare example of a burial associated with a standing stone (Coflein, s.v. *Maen Llwyd Standing Stone*).

P3

The magician **Gwydion ap Dôn**, much of whose story is located in the vicinity of Dinas Dinlle and **Morfa Dinlle**, is well known from the Fourth Branch of *The Mabinogi*, as well as from poems in the *Book of Taliesin* and Triads 28 and 67 (LPBT 196, TYP 400-02). A mound inside the Dinas Dinlle hillfort is possibly a Bronze Age barrow.

Defeillon is otherwise unknown. The third line is obscure. *Carannog* is an adjective meaning 'dear, beloved', attested in the poetry of the Gogynfeirdd in the twelfth century. However, it is also known as a personal name, as in the place name Llangrannog. A **Garannog** with the epithet *Glewddigar* (brave-angry) is recorded in some early genealogical tracts and referenced in a poem by the fourteenth-century poet, Gruffudd ap Maredudd ap Dafydd (WCD 269).

P4

The meaning of the first line is uncertain. **Credig** may be a syncopated form of *Ceredig*, but if so, we have here no way to know which, if any, of various figures with that name might be meant (see WCD 123-25).

P5-8

The four stanzas naming **Llofan Llaw Ddifo**, with his multiple epithets, suggest there may have been a tale about him of some note. A tradition reflected in Triad 33, 'Three Unfortunate Assassinations of the Island of Britain', states that it was Llofan who killed Urien ap Cynfarch (the father of Owain; Sts 13, 14), and in the Urien poems he is named *Llofan Law Ddifro* 'Llofan with the Hand of an Exile/Outlaw'. Difro may be the earlier form, on which *difo* is perhaps a pun or play. The general sense of *difo* is something along the lines of 'destruction, destructive';

Thomas Jones translates it as 'Murderous' (TJ 135), Rachel Bromwich as 'Severing' (TYP, Triad 33). **Llawygyn** in St P6 might be understood as *Llawengyn* 'with the Hand of a Knave/Outcast' (compare *Llwch Llawengin*, St 31). For Rowland's discussion of the growth and implications of the tradition of Llofan as Urien's assassin, see EWSP 114-17.

The very similar lines P5c and P6c are of uncertain meaning.

P7
Lines b and c of this stanza are identical to those of St P13, which is itself a variant of St 4.

P9
See the notes to St 10, of which this is a variant.

P10
See the notes to St 35, of which this is a variant.

P11
Benhych, Agen ap Rhugri (Ywgri?), **Ager**, and **Aber Bangori** are otherwise unknown.

P12
Both the poetic structure and the meaning of this fragment are obscure.

P13
Compare St P7 and see the notes to St 4, of which this is a variant.

P14
With **Disgyrnin Disgyffeddod** compare *Disgyfdawt* (TYP, Triads 10, 32). In accordance with the corrected MS reading, TJ prints *cigleu*, which could represent either the 1st or 3rd person preterite of *clywed* 'hear', and he interprets it as 1st person, which in this context is the more likely.

P15
Elidir Mwynfawr (the Wealthy) was a sixth-century contemporary of Urien Rheged and Rhydderch Hael in the Old North. Traditions about him have survived in several early sources. His horse was one of the 'Three Horses who carried the Three Horse-Burdens':

> *Black Moro, horse of Elidir Mwynfawr, who carried on his back seven and a half people from Penllech in the North to Penllech in Môn. These were the seven people: Elidir Mwynfawr and Eurgain his wife, daughter of Maelgwn Gwynedd, and Gwyn Good Companion, and Gwyn Good Distributor, and Mynach Naomon his counsellor, and Prydelaw the Cupbearer, his butler, and Silver Staff his servant, and Gelbeinvein his cook, who swam with his two hands to the horse's crupper – and that was the half person.*
> (TYP, Triad 44)

It was his status as the son-in-law of Maelgwn Gwynedd, who died about 547, that led Elidir to mount an expedition perhaps to claim the rule of Gwynedd after Maelgwn's death. The mid-thirteenth-century *Black Book of Chirk* law text (NLW Peniarth MS 29) includes a passage recounting Rhun ap Maelgwn's success in defeating those who came to avenge Elidir's death *en Aber Meuhedus* (at Aber Meweddus) (see TYP 501 for the text and translation).

The **Meweddus**, or possibly *Mefeddus*, has been identified as the Afon Wefus, which runs into the Desach from Bron yr Erw, east of Clynnog (HW 168).

P16
The spelling **Nanllau** represents a spoken form of *Nantlle*.

The name **Mabon ap Mydron** (or *Modron*) derives etymologically from the earlier names of the god **Maponos* and his mother **Matrona*. Though Mabon is not mentioned in *The Mabinogi*, Professor Eric Hamp has posited a relationship between *Mabon ap Modron* and the word *Mabinogi*, which he interprets as 'material relating to the story of Mabon'. Might, therefore, the location of Mabon's grave in Nantlle be a further reflection of some distant connection to *The Mabinogi*? Certainly the region around Nantlle plays a significant role, especially in the Fourth Branch. The same region is also referenced in Sts P3, P7, and P10, which names other characters from the same branch. A different narrative appears in the tale of *How Culhwch Got Olwen* in which the imprisoned Mabon is rescued by Arthur's men and assists in the hunt for the boar Twrch Trwyth. Mabon is also named as a companion of Arthur in the poem *Pa ŵr yw'r porthor?* (Who is the porter?), and as one of Arthur's counsellors in the *Dream of Rhonabwy*.

P17

Bedd anap lleian: The beginning of this englyn as written by Dr. Davies, the scribe of Peniarth 98B, appears to name the occupant of the grave: *Bedd Ann ap lleian* (The grave of Ann son of a nun). In Geoffrey of Monmouth's *History of the Kings of Britain*, the magicians of Gwrtheyrn Gwrthenau (see St 40) tell the king that his inability to build a sturdy castle can only be remedied with the blood of a boy with no father. This leads to the discovery of such a boy, who confounds the king's counsellors and solves the king's problem. In a fourteenth-century manuscript of *Brut y Brenhinedd*, a Welsh translation of Geoffrey's work, is a sentence that does not appear in Geoffrey's Latin: *Ac an ab y lleian y gelwit y mab kyn no hynny. Ac o hynny allan y dodet arnaw Merdyn. o achaws y gaffael yngkaer vyrdyn*. A fifteenth-century text similarly reads *an ap y lleian*. The editor, J. J. Parry, translates this as 'And up to that time he was called An, son of the Nun, and after that he was named Myrddin because he was found in Carmarthen [Caer Vyrdyn]' (BB 124). However, the likely underlying reading is *anap y lleian*, 'the misfortune/mishap (i.e., illegitimate child) of the nun', from *anap, anhap* (misfortune, misery, mishap, injury, loss). Such a reading is supported by the fact that whereas Geoffrey's text names the boy Merlinus as soon as he is discovered, the Welsh translation withholds his name until the boy has bested Gwrtheyrn's magicians and then gives this explanation. Dr. Davies, William Salesbury, the poet Lewys Glyn Cothi, and others read the phrase as a proper name, *An ap (y) lleian*, though Lewys seems also have been aware of the usage *anap ei fam* (his mother's misfortune). A further extension of this identification as a name leads to An(n) being identified as the 'chief magician of Myrddin Emrys', rather than as **Myrddin Emrys** himself (see Sims-Williams, "anfab[2] "illegitimate child": a ghost word').

P18

This incomplete and corrupt stanza is a variant of St 24.

Wrexham MS 1

W1

Wrexham MS 1 was written in the hand of John Brooke of Mucklewick, Shropshire, and Mawddwy, Merionethshire, in 1590-91. A lone grave stanza is accompanied by a marginal note: *hwn a gladdwyd mewn lle a elwir maes y kaerav yn emyl Dinas Embrys* (He was buried in a place called Maes y Caerau beside Dinas Emrys). The name **Gwryd** is a variant of *Cywryd* (see St 1). An alternative location might be Bryn Beddau, Clocaenog, near Ruthin in North Wales, with a cluster of four cairns (now lost to forestry). Another is Bryn y Beddau, Blaenrheidol, Ceredigion, whose name ('hill of the graves') may relate to cairns or barrows now submerged below Nant y Moch reservoir.

St P15 Cefngraianog stone, on the banks of the Desach, near the confluence with the Wefus

St 26 A misty Epynt sunset

Afterword: The Text and Context of *Englynion y Beddau*

The *Black Book of Carmarthen* is a small manuscript of about 5 inches by 7 inches with 108 pages, whose modest appearance belies its importance in the history of Welsh literature. There are earlier poems in later manuscripts, especially the twelve poems attributed to the historical poet Taliesin and the elegiac stanzas of *The Gododdin* of Aneirin, as well as a small number of individual poems found in the margins of earlier Latin manuscripts, but the *Black Book* is the oldest known collection of Welsh poetry. It was compiled around the middle of the thirteenth century by a single scribe, probably from the Carmarthen Priory of St John and Teulyddog, from which the manuscript was rescued at the dissolution of the monasteries in the sixteenth century. Into this small book the scribe copied a miscellany of some forty poems. These poems, from the twelfth century and earlier, range from prophecy and legendary history to praise poetry, elegy, and religious meditation. As Daniel Huws has pointed out, the scribe/compiler of the manuscript seems to have been 'guided by personal taste, he was working for himself, with no clear preconception of what his book would contain …. We might say that the impulse was literary rather than antiquarian'. In other words, the *Black Book* appears to be a collection of poetry of interest to an individual – indeed, a 'headstrong eccentric', to quote Daniel Huws again – rather than a collection of historical literary artifacts commissioned by a patron (MWM 71-2).

The connection with Carmarthen would seem to account for the scribe's interest in poetry attributed to Myrddin (known in English as Merlin), whose name was believed, incorrectly, to be the eponym for that of the town, *Caerfyrddin*. The *Black Book* opens, in a rather dramatic script, with an eleventh-century poetic dialogue between Myrddin and Taliesin, the second great poet-prophet of Welsh tradition, and there are three more prophetic poems in Myrddin's voice addressed respectively to a birch tree, an apple tree, and a little pig (see RoM 19-30). In addition, the scribe's interest extended more broadly to poems drawing on the legendary Welsh past. Here, for example, are some of the earliest and most important sources for our knowledge of Arthur prior to the rise of the great Welsh, Latin, French, German, and English Arthurian tales of the later Middle Ages (see RoA 11-16). There are also several poems in praise of important historical figures of the twelfth century – one anonymous poem each to Cuhelyn Fardd, lord of Cemais (c. 1100 – 30), and Hywel ap Goronwy, ruler of Deheubarth (d. 1106), and three poems by Cynddelw Brydydd Mawr (the Great Poet): one to the Lord Rhys of Deheubarth (1155 – 97), an elegy lamenting the death in 1160 of Madog ap Maredudd, the last ruler of a united Powys, and a series of five englynion addressed to Madog's household troops.

Among the poems drawing on or reflecting the traditional history of the Welsh are the verses that are the subject of this book, *Englynion y Beddau / The Stanzas of the Graves*. The scribe did not include that title, but a later hand has written *Englynnionn y Beddau* in the upper margin of the page on which the text begins. A more explicit title sometimes used is *Beddau Milwyr Ynys Prydain* (The Graves of the Warriors of the Island of Britain). *The Stanzas of the Graves* consist of seventy-three stanzas, all but one of which are *englynion* (sg. *englyn*), three- or four-line epigrammatic stanzas composed according to specific rules. Typically each stanza names one or two ancient heroes and in many cases gives the location of the grave site.

The seventy-three stanzas in the *Black Book* contain about ninety personal names, depending on how we count possible duplicates such as Owain, Cynon, and Rhun, and irregular forms such as *mab Osfran* (Osfran's son) and *unben o Bryden* (a chieftain of Pictland). Allowing for similar ambiguities, there are about fifty-six place names. All of the personal names that we can identify – and hence probably the ones we cannot – are legendary heroes from the fifth to the ninth century. Many are warriors from *yr Hen Ogledd* (the Old North), comprising the Brythonic or Cymric kingdoms in what is now northern England and southern Scotland. As Anglo-Saxons and Danes seized control over these regions, the traditions of former kings and heroes migrated to Wales and became an important part of the Welsh cultural memory. Others are known from the deep past in Wales itself. There are references to many of these figures in other poems, tales, triads, and traditions; some indeed are known quite well from tales that spread from Wales throughout Britain and Europe. Among these are characters who were drawn into the great cycle of Arthurian tales – Arthur, Owain, Gwalchmai (Gawain), March (Mark), Cynon, and Gwrtheyrn (Vortigern). A few are familiar from the great Welsh classic, *The Mabinogi* – Pryderi, Dylan, Lleu Llaw Gyffes, and possibly Llwyd. About twenty of the personal names, however, are known only from the *Stanzas of the Graves* themselves, some of them in intriguing references that hint tantalizingly at the existence of a tale now lost. Meigen ap Rhun and Beidog the Red, for instance, are each named in three consecutive stanzas (Sts 17 – 19, 36 – 38), suggesting that they may have been well known.

These names and tales, often relocated from distant places or from the mists of far earlier mythologies, became integral parts of both the historical memory and the landscape of Wales. Eight names, for instance, can also be found among the elegies of *The Gododdin*, celebrating the heroes who died at the battle of Catraeth about the year 600. Three of these were very likely taken directly from that poem (see St 3). Prominent among other heroes from the 'Old North' is Owain ab Urien (St 13), a prince of the kingdom of Rheged in the sixth century for whom the historical Taliesin composed an elegy and who plays an important role in later Arthurian legend. In the same englyn we meet Rhydderch Hael, a sixth-century king of Strathclyde who became one of the three paragons of generosity (TYP Triad 2). Rhydderch, Owain's father Urien, and Gwallog Hir (St 7), are all named in the ninth-century *Historia Brittonum* as kings who fought against Hussa, a sixth-century Anglo-Saxon king of Bernicia. Other notables from the Old North are Caw, Gwrgi, Gyrthmwl, Einion ap Cunedda, and Elidir Mwynfawr (Sts 1, 28, 39, 72, P15).

The Qualities of a Warrior

The heroic qualities of the men celebrated throughout the *Stanzas of the Graves* make up a fairly thorough listing of the ideal attributes of warriors who aspire to be, like Cynon ap Clydno, 'honored in verse' (St 9) and thereby to achieve some measure of lasting fame after death. They must, of course, be steadfast, brave, dauntless, fearless (Sts 20, 32, 53, 54), and fierce in battle (Sts 11, 22, 63, 66). Aron ap Dyfnwyn, for example, would prefer to hunt down a thief singlehandedly rather than call for help, and 'he would not give mercy to his enemies' (St 59). Of one unnamed hero with 'the ferocity of a wild boar' it is said with unnerving directness that *tra'th laddai chwarddai wrthyd* (as he killed you, he would laugh at you) (St 49). Animal imagery, though rare in this text, is also applied to Ceri Long-sword, who is *tarw torment* (bull of a host) (St 5), and Llwyd the Gentle and another unnamed hero (Sts 66, 69) are each described as *tarw trin* (bull of battle), a phrase that appears twice elsewhere in the *Black Book*, as well as several times in *The Gododdin*. *Tarw* (bull) is one of the most common metaphors for a warrior throughout medieval Welsh poetry. Warriors should stand firm in battle, like a bulwark or pillar (Sts 21, 22, 58), and retreat is out of the question (Sts 25, 27, 35, 48). We are reminded, too, of the close relationship between warriors and their horses (Sts 14, 15, 47, 63).

Other desirable qualities reflect the role of a leader when not at war. He should have 'lofty wisdom' (St 6) and be just, like Meigen ap Rhun, 'lord of right', and Brwyno the Tall, 'Strong his justice in his land' (Sts 19, 48). And as is frequently stated in medieval Welsh verse, he should be generous, like Rhydderch Hael (the Generous), Ffyrnfael Hael, and Talan Talyrth – 'bountiful, his gates open' (Sts 13, 33, 52).

While most of the figures named are men, four women are named as lying in 'the graves on the Morfa' (St 70). It may or may not be a coincidence that this is also the only stanza that is not in englyn form; rather it is in the ancient metre known as *awdl-gywydd* (see the 'Brief Note on Metre' below). The term *morfa* 'sea strand, marsh, salt-marsh, moor' is common in Wales, especially in coastal areas, but the particular *morfa* of this stanza is undoubtedly *Morfa Rhianedd* (sea strand of the maidens) on the north coast at Llandudno. Three of the four women and the one man named in this stanza have clear connections with the immediate area. Sanant, born in the sixth century into the royal dynasty of Powys, became the first wife of Maelgwn Gwynedd, whose court was not far off at Degannwy. Though Maelgwn himself is not named in any grave stanza, he did have, perhaps by his second wife, a son named Rhun, who is named here. As well as appearing in the *Triads of the Island of Britain* as one of Arthur's three mistresses (TYP Triad 57), Garwen was the daughter of Henyn Henben, who is celebrated in the stanza immediately following and who is named in the story of Taliesin as the chief poet of Maelgwn Gwynedd. At the east end of Morfa Rhianedd is Little Orme's Head, where Lledin's name survives in the place name Creigiau Rhiwledin (the rocks of Lledin's hill).

Location and Landscape

A survey of the identifiable locations given for the graves is helpful not only for determining the geographic range of the *Stanzas of the Graves*, but also for shedding light on the nature of these englynion as a collection. We might first note that only three stanzas do not contain a personal name (Sts 29, 49, 69). Of these, St 29 is linked, by its reference to Gwanas, to the preceding englyn, which places Gwrgi and Llawr 'in the uplands of Gwanas Gwŷr'; St 49 may have lost its name through textual corruption; and St 69 is an englyn whose opening question, 'Whose is the grave on yonder slope?', is answered only with the descriptive metaphor *tarw trin* (a bull of battle). Thus, one or more personal names is the norm in a grave stanza. On the other hand, thirty-five stanzas – nearly half of the total – contain no specific location. This strongly suggests that identifying the location of the graves of traditional heroes is not a primary purpose of these englynion. Conversely, we might counter with the argument that the inclusion of nearly sixty specific place names (eleven stanzas name more than one place) indicates that place is certainly an important element.

This importance might be to demonstrate the thorough knowledge of the imagined speaker, presumably the legendary Taliesin. However, it is also true that place is significant because it anchors in the landscape the traditions of the past that underlie the medieval Welsh concept of who is Welsh and what is Wales. Such a geographical function of *The Stanzas of the Graves* is consistent with current interpretations of the archaeological record. For example, in a brief overview of the contexts for early medieval inscribed stones in Wales, Nancy Edwards notes (Edwards, *Early-Medieval Inscribed Stones*, 23),

> *By the 9th or 10th century, when the verses of the Welsh poem* Englynion y Beddau *('Stanzas of the*

Graves') were brought together, it is clear that prominent prehistoric monuments, such as standing stones and cairns, were explained as the graves of mythical heroes and it seems likely that at least some of these associations may go back much further, in which case it is possible that 'ancestors' in the mythical past were being used to legitimise the present.... In this light it may be argued that the functions of the inscribed stones, which either use or are set against a backdrop of earlier monuments, often in prominent locations, are not merely commemorative, but also seem to act as written proof of entitlement to the surrounding land and its resources apparently since ancient times.

The identifiable places in the *Stanzas of the Graves* are distributed widely across the broad sweep of virtually the entire Welsh landscape. This suggests that whoever composed or brought together the *Stanzas of the Graves* as we have them in the *Black Book* text had a sense of Welsh cultural unity, even in the absence of political unity. It is during the same general period in which these stanzas were composed that the word *Cymry* begins to appear in the written record to designate 'the Welsh' and 'Wales'. The earliest certain examples are found in the hortatory prophecy *Armes Prydain*, composed sometime before the Battle of Brunanburh in 937. *Cymry* occurs thirteen times in that poem, which calls for an alliance with other enemies of the Anglo-Saxon king Athelstan in order to drive the Anglo-Saxons from Britain and restore the Britons' ancient rights and lands. If, as seems likely, the poem to Cadwallon ap Cadfan surviving in a seventeenth-century manuscript can be dated to the seventh century, the examples of *Cymry* there become the earliest (Gruffydd, 'Canu Cadwallon', pp. 27-28; Koch, *Cunedda*, pp. 199-203). While the word *Cymry* does not occur in the *Stanzas of the Graves* and there is no evidence of any overtly political or dynastic purpose in them, the vision of Wales embodied in the heroes' graves throughout the landscape is not inconsistent with a sense of cultural unity, if not 'nationhood', to use an anachronistic term, as is expressed in those two early poems, especially *Armes Prydain*.

The settings for the grave locations are also instructive. Only six of the *Black Book* graves mentioned are situated in or near a churchyard or *llan* (Sts 4, 5, 8, 13, 14, 50), and of these, Sts 13 and 14 may name competing sites for the grave of Owain ab Urien, though two different Owains may have been intended originally. Nor does a location at a *llan* (Llanfeuno, Llanbadarn, Llanforfael, Llanhiledd, Llanelwy) necessarily mean that the hero is actually buried in the church or churchyard. The sole exception is Ceri Longsword, who is explicitly said to be 'in the lowland of Heneglwys ... in Corbre's burial ground' (St 5). The secular nature of these stanzas is fully consistent with the heroic, traditional, and narrative origins of the lore which they preserve, however briefly. As in the poetry of the historical Taliesin, the elegies in *The Gododdin*, and other early Welsh verse, the descriptive emphasis is on the ferocity, bravery, and honourable death in battle of these warriors. Though the *Stanzas of the Graves* were composed in a Christian context, there is only the barest hint of the Christian view of death or life after death. This comes in St 69, which concludes *Tarw trin. Trugaredd iddaw!* (A bull of battle. Mercy to him!) There is no mention of God, and only one mention of fate in St 64.

Nine stanzas name sites on a hill (*bryn, bre, rhiw*) or mountain (*mynydd*), and four others are more generally situated in the uplands (*gwarthaf, gwrthdir, gorthir*). The most common locations, however, are burial sites near water. Five stanzas locate their graves at a ford (Sts 10, 24, 36, 55, 71), and seven others locate graves near the shore (4, 6, 7, 17-18, 50, 70). By far the most common setting is

St 70 Creigiau Rhiwledin

by a river. No fewer than seventeen streams or rivers are named. Often these are quite small streams, like the Gwenoli, named as Pryderi's burial place in St 7. The Gwenoli runs into the Prysor near the ford of Y Felenrhyd, where the Prysor joins the Dwyryd, just downstream from Maentwrog. Thus St 7 differs from, but is not necessarily inconsistent with, the account of Pryderi's burial in the Fourth Branch of *The Mabinogi*: 'And in Maen Tyfiawg, above Y Felenrhyd, he was buried, and his grave is there' (Mab 88).

Another minor stream is the Gefel or Gefail, named in St 26 as the place where a certain Epynt is said to be buried. Epynt may be, as Thomas Jones surmises, a personal name derived from the place name Epynt (horse track, horse path), for the Afon Gefail flows off Mynydd Epynt to join the Dulas near Llanwrtyd Wells. Whether there was a tradition about a hero named Epynt or this is a fanciful stanza drawing on unfamiliar names that were found to occur together may never be known. Another personal name derived from a place name is that of Taflogau in St 60, for this was an early form of the name of two streams, now called the Dologau or Nant Gau and the Logau Las, both of which flow into the Ystwyth. That Taflogau had become or was thought of as a character about whom a tale was told is suggested by the fact that he is given a patronym of considerable mythological note, Taflogau ap Lludd.

The identification of the river Peryddon in St 8 has been the subject of much research and speculation, for the name comes up in several medieval sources, including the tenth-century prophetic poem *Armes Prydain* and Welsh versions of Geoffrey of Monmouth's twelfth-century *History of the Kings of Britain*. The connection between Peryddon and Gwalchmai leads Patrick Sims-Williams to speculate that Peryddon may have been an early name for the stream at Sandyhaven Pill in Pembrokeshire, which flows from Castell Gwalchmai / Walwyn's Castle into Aberdaugleddau (AW 49-50).

'A grave for Arthur'

The englyn most often cited in modern times is perhaps St 44, which raises one of the great questions about the fate of Arthur – Did he die? The first two lines of this stanza state simply but firmly that graves exist for March, Gwythur, and Gwgon Gleddyfrudd. It is perhaps not coincidental that all three are associated in one place or another with Arthur. March is the husband of Essyllt (Isolde) and a key figure in the tale of Trystan (Tristan). Gwythur's name is again rhymed with Arthur in the 'Song of the Horses' in the book of Taliesin, and he is one of Arthur's men in the tale of *How Culhwch Got Olwen*. Gwgon Gleddyfrudd, who may in life have been a ninth-century king of Ceredigion, is named as a messenger to Owain ab Urien during Owain's game of *gwyddbwyll* with Arthur in *The Dream of Rhonabwy*. Patrick Sims-Williams puts forward the suggestion that because these three figures are all well-known from the Triads and other tales, this stanza may be 'relatively late' (AW 49). Another argument suggesting a late date might be the conjunction of Arthurian connections in this one stanza, though it is hard to know how early various characters may have been drawn into the gravitational field of Arthur's orbit.

In this englyn there are no qualifying words attesting to the prowess of these three men, nor any attempt to locate their graves. The bare fact that they have graves can only be to provide a contrast with the third line of the stanza: *Anoeth byd, bedd i Arthur*. Key to interpreting this line is the rare word *anoeth*. The meaning of *anoeth* is made clear, as it happens, by Arthur himself in the tale of Culhwch. The giant Ysbyddaden stipulates that in order to marry his daughter, Olwen, the young Culhwch must accomplish a number of impossible tasks and obtain various items that the giant expects will be impossible to get. Arthur refers to these objects and tasks collectively as *anoetheu*:

> *Arthur a dywawt, 'Pa beth yssyd iawnaf y geissaw gyntaf o'r annoetheu hynny?'*

> Arthur asked, 'What is most fitting to seek first of those things hard to find.'
> (CO 827; CT 45)

He asks a similar question three more times, always using this same word, and when all the tasks have been accomplished we are told,

> *Ac yna y kychwynnwys Kulhwch, a Goreu uab Custennin gyt ac ef, … a'r anoetheu gantunt hyt y lys.*

> And then Culhwch, and Gorau son of Custennin with him, … with the things hard to find, set out for his court.
> (CO 1232; CT 70).

Thus, we can with some confidence translate the third line of St 44 as 'A thing hard to find in the world, a grave for Arthur'. But a certain ambiguity remains. Does this mean that Arthur's grave is in a place that is hard to get to? That he was buried secretly and no one now knows where? Or that Arthur does not have a grave? And if the last, why not? Perhaps the closest we can come to an answer is to consider this englyn in the light of evidence from the early twelfth century. Around 1125 the chronicler William of Malmesbury wrote, 'The sepulchre of Arthur is nowhere to be seen, whence ancient ballads fable that he is still to come' (*Chronicle* 315). Similarly, in the 1140s Herman of Tournai recounted a journey made by some canons of Laon to Cornwall in 1113. During this journey a quarrel arose between the travelers and a Cornishman with a withered arm who insisted that Arthur was still alive, *sicut Britones solent jurgari cum Francis pro rege Arturo* (just as the Bretons were wont to quarrel with the French about King Arthur) (AW 262). Clearly a belief that Arthur did not die was current in Wales, Brittany, and Cornwall by the early twelfth century. It would seem that St 44 reflects a similar tradition at an earlier date, though we cannot be positive that this particular englyn is as early as the ninth or tenth century.

We should note, however, that there are also traditions around Wales which attach Arthur's name to possible grave sites. Excluding such monuments as the several Neolithic chambered tombs known as *Coetan Arthur* 'Arthur's Quoit', whose names reflect tales about Arthur lightly tossing their capstones into place, and not counting pieces of Arthurian household furniture such as *Bwrdd Arthur* (Arthur's table), *Cadair Arthur* (Arthur's chair), *Ffynnon Cegin Arthur* (Arthur's kitchen well), there are various cairns, cromlechs, and stone circles that bear his name. The most evocative of these is the 'explicitly ambiguous monument' (*Coflein*, s.v. *Bedd Arthur*) known as *Bedd Arthur* in Pembrokeshire, a Neolithic or Bronze Age stone circle comparable to the oval of bluestones at Stonehenge, quarried nearby. The name *Bedd Arthur* alone may seem to put the lie to St 44, though of course we do not know when that name was first applied to these stones. *Maen Ceti* in the Gower has been known as Arthur's Stone at least since the seventeenth century. To these we might add the *Glyn Arthur* and *Craig Arthur* cairns, the *Cerrig Arthur* stone circle, and *Coed Maen Arthur* (The wood of Arthur's stone).

Form and Structure

The structure of the *Stanzas of the Graves* is flexible. That is to say, the specific order of the stanzas is not important, except in a few cases in which information for understanding one stanza is found in a preceding one. For example, St 47 is not a grave stanza, strictly speaking, but it gives further information as to the identities of Eiddew and Eidal named in St 46. Similarly, Sts 17-19 and Sts 36-38, honouring Meigen ap Rhun and Beidog Rudd, respectively, form chains that naturally go together. These short series allow us to see some of the subtleties of the englyn form, in which the slight variation and incremental repetition in each stanza take us deeper into our understanding of what kind of men Meigen and Beidog were, as we ponder the situation they are in, literally and figuratively. Meigen lies near the shore and aspects of his lordship are referenced in the final rhyme of each stanza – he is lord of a hundred, lord of a court, and finally and perhaps most importantly, a lord of justice. Line 19b, 'in the track of Amir's host' may refer to an episode from a lost tale about Meigen; alternatively, it may recall an unrelated event that identifies the location of his burial to those who understand the reference. The second and third Beidog stanzas, on the other hand, lead us not back to Beidog in life, but to a stark consideration of his fate, taking us into the grave itself where his bones lie hidden, reminding us that we too shall be separated from our deeds and our worldly possessions. In another chain,

Sts 21-23 provide specific identifying information about Môr and Meilyr and Madog, who are named without elaboration in St 20.

Other stanzas are linked together through verbal or metrical devices that have little to do explicitly with the subject of each stanza. The most common method is to repeat the first word or phrase in successive stanzas, a linking device known as *cymeriad geiriol* (verbal linking). For instance, twenty-nine of the thirty-two stanzas beginning with the key word *bedd* 'grave' are linked with a least one other; the longest such chain is five stanzas in length, Sts 50-54. Fourteen of the twenty stanzas beginning *Piau'r bedd …?* (Whose is the grave …?) are similarly linked. This device provides a continuity of structure that is both varied and familiar.

The first three stanzas provide an excellent example of the poetic power of such linking, as well as illustrating the ways in which incremental repetition imbues them with cumulative meaning. They each begin with *Y beddau a …* (The graves which …); lines *a* and *b* are syntactically similar, and each line *c* consists of three names. None of the three mentions the location of their graves. It is the poetic structure of these opening stanzas that draws us into the series in terms of both the informational content and its underlying implications, thus raising the whole above the level of a mere catalogue of names and places. (For more on the metrical structure of the englynion, see *A Brief Note about Metre* below.)

Function and Meaning

It has long been a commonplace of commentary on the *Stanzas of the Graves* to say that they are antiquarian in purpose. Even though most scholars writing about the poem note briefly its poetic effect, it is often assumed that an important, even primary function of the *Stanzas of the Graves* is to serve as a mnemonic catalogue of traditional heroes. Jenny Rowland's comment is representative: 'As even a cursory examination of the *beddau* stanzas will show, these stanzas have an elegiac and lyric tone *despite their essential catalogue function*' (EWSP 55; my italics). The verses are seen as an aid to the memories of poets and storytellers, the keepers of traditional lore. In this regard these englynion are thought of as similar to such undoubted catalogues as are found in the *Triads of the Island of Britain* and other texts.

The triads, however, are prose listings, not verse. It is true, of course, that the *Stanzas of the Graves* contain much information that is of antiquarian interest, not just to us but to the original audience as well. But is that the whole story? In the *Stanzas of the Graves* there is no such regularity of style and structure as we might expect of a catalogue *per se*. Lists of names are not uncommon in early Welsh poetry, and they can be quite interesting in their own right. For example, the early Arthurian poem also found in the *Black Book* and known from its first line as *Pa ŵr yw'r porthor?* (Who is the porter?) provides an intriguing early listing of characters, some of whom were drawn into the corpus of Arthurian tales that centuries later would become one of the greatest, and certainly the longest enduring cycle of tales in Europe. But even this early poem (incomplete in the manuscript, alas), has a narrative setting, though it may be largely lost to us. The later prose tales of *How Culhwch Got Olwen*, *The Dream of Rhonabwy*, and *Geraint* all contain catalogues that are undoubtedly meant to impress the audience while they also serve a function within the narrative. Indeed, as we know from other traditional literatures, from the *Iliad* of Homer to the Hawaiian epic *Kumulipo*, such lists serve an important literary purpose as well as a memorial one.

The *Stanzas of the Graves*, on the other hand, have no such progressive narrative content, however minimal. Insofar as they are replete with names and brief references to lore or tales of past heroes, they do bear a certain similarity to the *Triads of the Island of Britain*. Given that remembering and transmitting ancient and traditional lore was an important function of the early medieval poets, it is easy to see how the *Triads* served as a mnemonic device, using evocative key vocabulary terms (e.g., *gwyndeyrn* (fair prince), *post cad* (pillar of battle), *rhuddfoawg* (red ravager)) to classify and recall groups of names or events. The same is true of the legal triads and other triadic collections. But there are some important differences between these listings and the *Stanzas of the Graves*. A major distinction is the fact that the *Stanzas of the Graves* are in verse and they progress with a non-sequential thematic unity that imbues them with a resonance that extends beyond the simple, literal meaning of each *englyn* considered individually. To classify them as an antiquarian catalogue is to ignore the cumulative effect of these verses and to set aside the one overarching image that may be the *raison d'etre* for the whole: the grave itself. And in doing so we lose the poetry. The poet or compiler does not simply list names of past heroes and their burial places. Within the context of the heroic ethic, he focuses directly on the very fact of death, and he does so with a constantly shifting perspective and an array of sombre imagery ranging from the rain of the first stanza to the former pride of Beli ap Benlli in the last. However varied in life the heroic qualities and personal characteristics of all those named, there is an inescapable condition that they now share. Through the spare nature of the englyn with its terseness and its gradually shifting imagery, we are presented with an affective meditation on the ineluctable finality of death.

The very first line of *The Stanzas of the Graves* epitomizes the whole:

Y beddau a'u gwlych y glaw
The graves which the rain wets –

The subject, clearly, is 'graves', but it is the rain that evokes an atmosphere that is carried throughout all seventy-three englynion. The contemplation of graves, in and of itself, is enough to make us melancholy; the rain, however, reminds us that we are helpless to do anything to alleviate the fate of the dead who lie there. The second line provides a context that heightens the effect of the first by revealing the sort of men who have died:

gwŷr ni ddyfnasynt hwy ddignaw:
men who were not used to being offended:

That is to say, men who were powerful, deserving of respect, not to be opposed. Yet here they lie. And the third line of this first englyn brings the message home to us with a specificity in triplicate:

Cerwyd a Chywryd a Chaw.
Cerwyd and Cywryd and Caw.

These are names the audience might be expected to know from tales, legends, and poems that preserve the past. But perhaps most significantly, these are individuals who, according to tradition, lived here on this earth, just as we live, and who died, just as in our turn, so shall we. This stanza and the two immediately following do nothing to locate the graves of their dead heroes. Rather through repetition and variation they draw us into a meditation on mortality. Simultaneously they begin an exploration of exemplary behavior based on the heroic code – the idealization of bravery and the glory to be gained from an honorable death in battle, though here repeatedly adumbrated by the eternal finality of death.

Warfare was frequent, if not constant, in the Heroic Age – for example, Llwch Llawengin 'would not be three months without battle' (St 31) – and it was through battle that a man could aspire to fame, both while he lived and afterwards. The composer(s) of these stanzas would almost certainly agree with the perspective summarized clearly in *The Gododdin* that 'Although they were slain, they slew, / And until the end of the world they shall be praised' (*Gododdin*, lines 867-8). But though these verses participate in perpetuating the memory of heroes of the past, the *Stanzas of the Graves* neither dwell on nor extol the fame that comes after death. Rather our attention is repeatedly drawn to the visible evidence of the permanence of death – the grave itself. Indeed, the word *bedd(au)* 'grave(s)' occurs 112 times in the 73 stanzas in the *Black Book*, and the numerous aspects of the graves described establish and maintain a mournful, meditative, often poignant tone throughout.

The first and third stanzas evoke the rain, while the second names the *gwyddwal*, the wild thicket or brambles that traditionally grow over an untended grave. (Here we might recall the briar that grows over the neglected grave of Culhwch's mother at the beginning of the tale of *How Culhwch Got Olwen* and even the greenbriar over the lovers' graves in some versions of the well-known ballad of *Barbara Allen*.) The grave of Elchwith is also wet by rain (St 45), and from a grave stanza recorded in the *Red Book of Hergest* we learn that 'there is thick snow on the grave of Eirinfedd' (St R4). Ceri Long-sword's grave is 'on the gravelly slopes' (St 5). Cynon may be buried *yn uchel tyddyn* 'in a high dwelling', but he rests nevertheless *yn isel gwelyddyn* (in a low bed) (St 9). Rhun ap Pyd lies *yn oerfel, yng ngweryd* (in the cold, in the earth) (St 10), and Rhun ab Alun Dyfed lies somewhat ignominiously *a'i ben gan yr anwaered* (with his head downhill) (St 24). Thomas Jones suggests this latter detail may be included primarily to provide a rhyme with Rhyd Faen-ced and Dyfed (St 24; TJ 112). However, it may rather be that the rhyme creates a more intense effect than would some similar statement in prose; that is, after all, an important function of poetry.

Three stanzas take us underground to consider the grave itself from the inside. The famed Owain ab Urien is constrained 'in a four-sided world / under the earth of Llanforfael' (St 13). *Ys cul y bedd ac ys hir* (Narrow and long is the grave) of Meigen ap Rhun, covered as well by sea, lowland, and thicket (Sts 17-19). These evoke images of chambered tombs and cist burials. Most jarring perhaps is the haunting image of the bones of Beidog the Red, far from the turmoil he caused and from his wealth, hidden by the earth of Machawy: *hirwynion bysedd Beidog Rudd* (long and white are the fingers of Beidog the Red) (Sts 37-8). Llia the Irishman, too, is described as hidden, expressing both the literal and concrete fact of burial and the separation of the dead from the world in which we, the audience of the poem, still live (St 26). Like Rhufawn, all of these men, presumably, were laid, 'too young in the earth' (St 43), and the grave of Llachar ap Rhun conjures up the profound quiet that engulfs them there: 'common was a corpse from his hand / before he was silent under stones' (St 51). The grave of Elsner ap Nêr 'in the depth of the earth' reminds us, too, that our time is short – *pen llu fu tra fu ei amser* (he was head of a host in his time) (St 53). A similar reminder of the shortness of our allotted time is expressed unequivocally in St 64 in proverbial form:

Lleas pawb pan ry dyngir.
Everyone's death comes when it is fated.

Death is a powerful and persistent theme in much early Welsh verse, which is perhaps not surprising in a time when societies were structured around an elite warrior aristocracy pledged to fight and die heroically in the service of a leader

'in a four-sided world' – Llety'r Filiast, Great Orme

who in return provides them with food, drink, and the spoils of war. This is a central theme of *The Gododdin*, a series of elegies for the warriors who died at the battle of Catraeth fighting against a much larger Anglo-Saxon host around the year 600. The saga englynion which preserve for us the outline of the tale of the aged Llywarch Hen raise questions about that heroic ideal as he mourns the loss of his twenty-four sons. In the poems of Heledd, the narrator laments the loss of her brothers in battle and the deaths of her sisters as their home in Powys is destroyed by war. In the poems of Urien, the poet laments the death of his lord, Urien of Rheged. Unlike the core of the *Gododdin* and the poems of the historical Taliesin, the poetic remains of these three surviving sagas are not historical poems written by poets who knew the characters and witnessed the events recounted. Rather they are imagined retellings composed some centuries later. As such they preserve for us not a historical record of events, but insight into the themes that were important to the poets themselves and their audiences.

Another series of seven englynion in the *Black Book* – possibly part of a poetic dialogue between Elffin's father Gwyddno Garanhir and the mythological otherworldly huntsman Gwyn ap Nudd – deals similarly with the theme of death, though no mention is made of either grave or location. They focus, rather, on the fact of death and the carnage after battle. Two images are repeated – the carrion crows that are referenced frequently in heroic poetry and the lament that the poet remains alive though these heroes are dead.

Mi a fûm yn y lle llas Gwenddolau
ap Ceidio, colofn cerddau,
ban ry reaint brain ar grau.

Mi a fûm yn lle llas Brân
ab Iwerydd clod lydan,
ban ry reaint brain garthan.

Mi a fûm lle llas Llachau
ab Arthur, uthr yng ngherddau,
ban ry reaint brain ar grau.

Mi a fûm lle llas Meurig
ap Careian clod edmig
ban ry reaint brain ar gig.

Mi a fûm lle llas Gwallog
mab gwehelyth teithïog,
adfod Lloegr, mab Lleynog.

Mi a fûm lle llas milwyr Prydain
  o'r dwyrain i'r gogledd.
  Myfi fyw. Wyntau ym medd.
Mi a fûm lle llas milwyr Prydain
  o'r dwyrain i'r deau.
  Myfi fyw. Wyntau yn angau.

I was where Gwenddolau was killed,
the son of Ceidio, pillar of songs,
when crows croaked over blood.

I was where Brân was killed,
the son of Iwerydd, of widespread fame,
when carrion crows croaked.

I was where Llachau was killed,
the son of Arthur, terrible in songs,
when crows croaked over blood.

I was where Meurig was killed,
son of Careian, famed in praise,
when crows croaked over flesh.

I was where Gwallog was killed,
the son of a rightful lineage,
the affliction of Lloegr, son of Lleynog.

I was where the warriors of Britain were killed
  from the east to the north.
  I am alive. They are in the grave.

I was where the warriors of Britain were killed
  from the east to the south.
  I am alive. They are in death.

As with the *Stanzas of the Graves*, the warriors named in these englynion are from the Old North. The poet claims to have been present when each of these men was killed; thus these stanzas, too, express with confidence the narrator's command over the sort of knowledge of the past that a poet should have. Nevertheless, the most striking aspect of these verses is a sense of loss and the grief and loneliness of one whose companions and leaders have died.

The *Black Book* scribe also copied fourteen religious

poems into his manuscript. Much of this verse is anonymous and is generally simpler in language and style than the religious poetry of the *Gogynfeirdd*, the highly placed court poets of the Welsh princes in the twelfth and thirteenth centuries. The poem beginning *Moli Duw yn nechrau a diwedd* (Praise God in the beginning and the end), composed in the twelfth century or earlier, deals directly and descriptively with the coming of death. One passage in particular strikes a note that is perhaps more than a little reminiscent of the tone of the *Stanzas of the Graves*. After invoking Christ and Mary and asking for God's mercy, the poet continues,

> *Cyn myned i'm gweryd, i'm irfedd,*
> *yn dywyll, heb gannwyll, i'm gorsedd,*
> *i'm gweinfod, i'm gorod, i'm gorwedd,*
> *gwedy meirch ac ymddwyn glasfedd*
> *a chyfedd a chyd im â gwragedd,*
> *ni chysgaf – gobwyllaf o'm diwedd.*

> Before going to my earth, to my fresh grave,
> in darkness, without a candle, to my earthen mound,
> my narrow place, my hiding-place, my lying down,
> after horses and partaking of fresh mead
> and feasting and coupling with women,
> I will not sleep – I will consider my end.
>
> (See LlDC 13.12-17)

While there is no evidence of influence from the *Stanzas of the Graves* – though the phrase *gwedy meirch* (after horses) recalls Sts 14 and 15 – we might discern a commonality of imagery, tone, and topic in these poems that seems to have suited the taste of the *Black Book* scribe.

'Whose grave is this?'

Twenty of the stanzas open with the question *Piau'r bedd?* (Whose is the grave?). This question has a particular bearing on the status of those who lie buried, and it also suggests another reason for these verses to be remembered and recited. A triad found in the series of legal triads in the *Book of Blegywryd*, one of the rescensions of early Welsh law, reads,

> *Teir gwarthrut kelein ynt: gofyn 'Pwy a ladawd hwn?*
> *Pieu y bed hwn? Pieu yr elor hon?'*

> The three shames of a corpse are: asking 'Who killed this person? Whose grave is this? Whose bier is this?'
>
> (Bleg 116.3-5)

The legal distinctions differentiating these three question may originally have been to determine (1) Who (or whose family) is responsible for making recompense for this death? (2) Who is to be paid the compensation? and (3) Who is responsible for the burial arrangements? Not knowing the answers would clearly be shameful to the family of the dead. Given the repetition of the second of these questions in the *Stanzas of the Graves*, we might be able to broaden its implications in this poetic context. To get an answer to the question 'Whose grave is this?' is to establish the identity of the person buried and hence to determine the relationship, rights, and status of that person's descendants and relatives. The names given in reply are those of the heroes of past times. Assuming their tales, or even simply their existence, to be historically true, the presence of these ancient graves in the landscape becomes incontrovertible evidence of the right of their descendants, i.e., the Welsh as a people, to their land – Cymry (later Cymru), which can be understood etymologically as 'the land in which we live together'. Not to know who lies in these traditional burial sites would be shameful not only to the reputation of the one said to be buried there, it would also be shameful for those responsible for preserving and passing on that information. That responsibility lay in the poets and the storytellers, that is, the *cyfarwyddiaid*, who were more than storytellers – they were the living repositories of the traditional lore that identifies us to ourselves and that helps us, if we are Welsh, to understand who we are.

This perspective helps to clarify the function of three stanzas in particular. The reference to Elffin in Sts 42-43 makes it as clear as such things can be that the speaker of those two englynion, and probably by implication all the others, is imagined to be the legendary Taliesin, the all-knowing prophet-poet who had been set adrift as an infant in a coracle on the river Dyfi, only to be discovered by Elffin ap Gwyddno, who named him Taliesin and became his patron. (That the historical Taliesin was a sixth-century bard some of whose poems have survived is, in the way of such things, the hard evidence that the legend is 'based on a true story', as we might say today.) These two stanzas thus become perhaps our earliest evidence for the legendary 'Taliesin', as distinct from the historical one. Much of the poetry attributed to this 'Taliesin' is wisdom poetry, predicated on (or giving rise to) the tale of how he gained knowledge of the past, present, and future from the magic cauldron of Ceridfen as a boy (before he was subsequently reborn and set adrift). As he 'himself' states in the poem *Angar Kyfundawt*:

Mitwyf Taliessin:
ryphrydaf-y iawn llin;
 paräwt hyt ffin
yg kynelw Elphin.

* * *

Gogwn…
am detwyd dieu,
am buched ara,
am oesseu yscorua,
am haual teÿrned,
py hyt eu kygwara.

I am Taliesin:
I compose a [song of] impeccable pedigree;
my praise of Elffin
will last until Doom.

* * *

I know…
about propitious days,
about a joyful life,
about the aeons of the fortress,
about ones like kings,
how long their dwelling place [shall last].
(LPBT 112, 114)

The heroes named in the Stanzas of the Graves, if not kings in fact, were certainly 'ones like kings'. It is not unreasonable to assume that it is the same Taliesin-narrator who declares in St 46:

Piau'r bedd hwn? Bedd hwn a hwn?
Gofyn i mi. Mi a'i gwn.

Whose is this grave? This grave and this?
Ask me. I know it.

Any later poet who recites these stanzas and passes on this ancient lore, we might assume, participates in the unquestionable authority of Taliesin.

Names from *The Mabinogi*

Six, possibly seven, stanzas name characters from *The Mabinogi*. The references in general are so spare that there is little other than the mention of a name and place to connect these characters with the tales. It is clear from *The Mabinogi* itself that there were other tales, now lost, about Dylan eil Ton. There is no additional information about him in either St 4 or St P7, though the location at Llanfeuno makes it virtually certain that the same character is intended.

The location of Pryderi's burial at Aber Gwenoli in St 7 seems at first to be inconsistent with the version of the account of his death in the Fourth Branch. However, *yn Maen Tyuyawc, uch y Uelen Ryd* 'in Maentwrog, above Y Felenrhyd' in *The Mabinogi* might be understood to mean 'in [the vicinity of] Maentwrog, upstream from Y Felenrhyd on the Prysor', i.e., at Aber Gwenoli.

The description of the grave of Lleu Llaw Gyffes in St 35 might be interpreted in the light of his role in the Fourth Branch. It is tempting to see in the general location 'under the sea's shelter / where his kinsman was', or possibly 'where his shame was', a connection with his early life on the coast of Arfon in the vicinity of his eponymous Dinas Dinlle, the nearby Maen Dylan commemorating his twin brother, and the offshore location of the natural rock formation known as Caer Arianrhod, visible only at the lowest spring tides. In the tale his mother Aranrhod complains to Gwydion about the shame which she feels from the boy's mere existence, because of his mysterious birth when she was thought to be a virgin. She tries to prevent him from gaining public recognition or acceptance by denying him a name, arms, and a wife, although Gwydion assures her that 'if there be upon you no greater shame than that I have raised a boy as good as this, a small thing will your shame be' (Mab 95). Later Lleu's wife and her lover, Gronw Befr, nearly succeed in murdering him, and after his recovery Lleu insists on his legal right to compensation in the form of a tit-for-tat encounter with Gronw. Might a version of this be reflected in the line *Gŵr oedd hwnnw gwir i neb ni roddes* (That was a man who yielded right to no one)? However, nothing is said in *The Mabinogi* of the actual death of Lleu; the tale ends simply, 'Lleu Llaw Gyffes conquered the land a second time and ruled over it successfully. And as the tale says, he was lord of Gwynedd after that' (Mab 108).

The grave of Gwydion ap Dôn is also appropriately located on Morfa Dinlle, very near to where he takes part in the upbringing of Lleu Llaw Gyffes in *The Mabinogi*, but again there is nothing more in St P3 to shed any additional light on him or his story. It is perhaps worth noting that Dylan, Pryderi, Lleu, and Gwydion all appear in the Fourth Branch of *The Mabinogi*. Sir John Rhŷs's identification of Llwyd Llednais in St 66 with Llwyd ap Cil Coed is highly speculative; the epithet *llednais* 'courteous, well-behaved, temperate, kind(ly), gentle' does not particularly suggest the demeanor of Llwyd ap Cil Coed in the Third Branch.

The Compilation of Grave Stanzas in the *Black Book* and other sources

Sixty-nine stanzas were originally transcribed into the *Black Book*, and the scribe left half a page blank, turning over the leaf to begin the next poem. Four additional stanzas (Sts 70-73) were later added in the blank space, with a different ink and in a somewhat different orthography. Most noticeably, *bedd* and *beddau* 'grave(s)' (to give their modern forms) are here spelled *bed-beddeu*, rather than *bet-betev/beteu* as they invariably appear elsewhere. It was formerly believed that this addition was in an altogether different hand, but Daniel Huws has determined that it is the hand of the same scribe (see MWM 71). This suggests the likely passage of time indicated by the adoption of a newer orthographic style or perhaps an uncharacteristic instance in which the scribe did not adapt his copy text to his own earlier spelling practice. (The use of *dd* did not become widespread until sometime after the beginning of the fifteenth century, though it does appear sporadically earlier.) The addition of these four stanzas indicates that there were individual stanzas or perhaps strings or groupings of stanzas in oral or written tradition. This, coupled with the appearance of the stanzas found in other manuscripts as discussed below, raises the question of the composition of grave stanzas. The genre would seem to be an established one, at least in Celtic contexts, for there is a similar series of fifty-seven Old Irish quatrains 'On the Graves of the Men of Leinster' composed by the Irish cleric Broccán the Pious in the late tenth century (TJ 101-2).

Another collection of eighteen grave stanzas is found in NLW Peniarth MS 98B, transcribed by Dr. John Davies of Mallwyd in the early seventeenth century. This collection immediately follows a copy of the entire *Black Book*, and Davies includes a note stating, *Ychwaneg o Englynion y Beddau, o law Wiliam Salsbri, medd Rossier Morys.* (Additional *Englynion y Beddau*, from the hand of William Salesbury, says Roger Morris). Salesbury was a notable sixteenth-century scholar and translator of the New Testament, and Morris was a transcriber of manuscripts in the later part of that century. Thus Davies' note, copied out of Peniarth MS 111 (c. 1610), shows that his copy is at least four removes from Salesbury's source. As was done generally, Dr. Davies and his predecessors modernized the spelling of their transcriptions to a contemporary standard or their individual practice; nor were they averse to emending parts of a text that were not understood. Thus we can not know the precise readings of the original.

There are six cases of verbal or stylistic points of similarity between the stanzas in Peniarth 98B and those in the *Black Book*. There is no evidence of any direct link between these two sources, but their commonalities give us a glimpse into the ways in which variants may have been generated through oral transmission or during copying, either intentionally or accidentally. For example, St P1 is a close variant of St 33, except that the *Black Book* stanza is in question form, beginning *Piau'r y bedd yn y mynydd ... ?* (Whose is the grave on the mountain ...?), whereas the Peniarth 98B stanza is declarative, *Y bedd yn y gorfynydd ....* (The grave in the highland ...). In other respects their differences are merely orthographic. Though St P18 is too corrupt to allow us to reconstruct the full englyn, enough remains to recognize it as a variant of St 24, and here too they differ in their respective declarative and interrogative structures. There is no way to know which style is the innovation, though it is perhaps telling that none of the stanzas in the later manuscript are couched as questions. St P13 is a very close variant of St 4; St P7 is identical in lines *b* and *c*, though its line *a* is completely different. Conversely, Sts P10 and 35 have nearly identical first lines, while lines *b-c* differ. Thomas Jones comments that the evident 'textual confusion points to a long manuscript and oral tradition for the englynion'. Whether they are, as Jones states, 'at least as old as those in the Black Book', is less certain (TJ 99).

Five grave stanzas may also be found in the *Red Book of Hergest*, though here they do not stand alone as independent poems or a collection of englynion on a common theme. Rather they are included amongst the poems relating to Llywarch Hen and his sons (Sts R1-R3) and the laments of Heledd (Sts R4-R5). Thus these englynion give us some small insight into how such poetic lore could be embedded in a narrative context. Llywarch Hen was a sixth-century prince from the 'Old North' of Britain and a cousin of Owain's father, Urien (see St 13). Sometime around the mid ninth century, when the kingdom of Powys was suffering a period of adversity, a storyteller from there told a tale about Llywarch, the outlines of which survive in several series of englynion which were likely recited during key moments of the tale itself. Though these englynion about or spoken through the persona of Llywarch Hen do not tell the full story, the underlying narrative is clear: Llywarch the Old has outlived his many sons and he laments their loss and the role he played in encouraging them to go to battle. These are traditionally twenty-four in number and no fewer than twelve are named in this string of four stanzas (one of which is not a grave stanza per se). The Llywarch Hen saga poems are as much an examination – though not necessarily an outright rejection – of the assumptions of the heroic ethic as they are a poetic evocation of the realities of grief. It is not surprising that grave stanzas would find their way into, or perhaps even be explicitly composed for, this poetry of tragic loss.

The linked englynion of Sts R4 and R5 are found amongst the poems related through the persona of Heledd, though there is no recognizable connection between the two grave stanzas and the underlying narrative of those poems in which Heledd, a daughter of Cyndrwyn, a sixth-century ruler of Powys, laments the deaths of her brothers and sisters and the destruction of her home at Pengwern. Sts R4 and R5 are linked through the mention of Maes Maoddyn and through the syntactic similarity of the first lines. St R5 mentions an otherwise unidentified Cynon. Jenny Rowland offers a reasonable explanation of the presence of these englynion in the collection of Heledd poetry: 'These two stanzas are probably stray *beddau* stanzas, perhaps attracted by the name of Cynon, identified rightly or wrongly as Cynon mab Cyndrwyn' (EWSP 610). St R5 is a variant of St 45 in the *Black Book*.

Unfortunately, neither can we know the ultimate source of the eighteen stanzas in Peniarth MS 98B. They appear in early modern antiquarian contexts, and we do not know whether William Salesbury or his source collected them from a variety of manuscripts or found them as a series in a single source. The best (indeed the only) evidence we have – the poems themselves and their Irish analogues – suggests that the *Stanzas of the Graves* are most likely to have been composed as one or more series of englynion, to which additional stanzas might be added and from which others might be borrowed (or imitated), as may be the case with the five stanzas in the *Red Book*. Whatever their source or sources, the cumulative emotional effect and poetic power of the series in the *Black Book* is clearly evident. In this light, we can only agree with William Bingley's assessment of the *Stanzas of the Graves* in 1804 in his description of his visits to North Wales, and we fervently hope that his prediction continues to prove true:

"Beddau Milwyr Ynys Prydain," *The Tombs of the Warriors of Britain*, is a noble piece of antiquity, and will last while the country and the language exist.
(Bingley 128)

A Brief Note on Metre

With a single exception, each of the seventy-three stanzas in the *Black Book* is in one or another of several early forms of *englyn* (pl. *englynion*). The varieties of englyn comprise a deceptively simple form. The englyn poet has command over a number of structural, metrical, and verbal devices and elements that move us from one line to the next and from one stanza to another, creating a poetic continuity for the whole without an explicit narrative or thematic structure. Even the relatively simple types of englynion found in these early texts have a sophistication that presages the increasing complexities of Welsh verse in later centuries. The origins and development of the englyn have been subjects of much debate, commentary, and research which need not be rehearsed here; the following descriptions are greatly simplified. (The classic study of Welsh metrics is John Morris-Jones's *Cerdd Dafod* [1925], and an excellent source of information in English is Jenny Rowland's extensive *Early Welsh Saga Poetry: A Study and Edition of the 'Englynion'* [1991].)

The underlying form may have been the *englyn milwr* (warrior's englyn), also formerly called an *englyn tair awdl* (three rhyme englyn). Both terms are known from the sixteenth century (GP 113, 179). The *englyn milwr* is defined as having three rhyming lines of seven syllables. However, in the early period the number of syllables was not quite as firmly fixed as it later became, and there is considerable variation in the poetry at hand. Thirty-one of the *Black Book* stanzas are *englynion milwr*, and of these only fifteen have seven syllables in all three lines, as in St 8, for example. One should keep in mind, too, that because of ambiguities in textual readings, orthography, scribal error, etc., it is not always possible to determine the number of syllables in a line with complete certainty; the descriptions given here are based as much as possible on stanzas about which there is minimal doubt.

The *englyn penfyr* (short-headed englyn) is a somewhat more complex and variable structure that may have developed from the *englyn milwr*. The *englyn penfyr* has three lines, of which line *a* is lengthened and *b* and *c* invariably rhyme. Line lengths are typically 10-6-7 or 11-6-7 syllables, though only about a third of the thirty-seven grave stanzas in this metre have all three lines of these lengths. The structure and ornamentation of internal rhyme and alliteration in line *a* varies considerably, as does the amount and patterning of alliteration and internal rhyme throughout each stanza. In sixteen of these stanzas a word before the end of line *a* rhymes with lines *b-c* and is followed by another word or words that end the line, often rhyming with a word in the middle of line *b*. In fifteen stanzas line *a* contains no rhyme at all. In some stanzas, the two halves of line *a* rhyme; elsewhere the first half of line *a* rhymes with a non-final word in the second half.

Two stanzas, Sts 46 and 72, are *englynion gwastad*. The *englyn gwastad* (level englyn) is essentially an *englyn milwr* with a fourth seven-syllable rhyming line. As noted above, the syllable count is not absolute; lines 46a and 72b each have eight syllables.

Two further stanzas, Sts 32 and 65, are perhaps best described as nascent *englynion cyrch*. The *englyn cyrch* (attacking or moving englyn) is a four-line stanza with seven syllables per line. Lines *a-b-d* have the same end rhyme, while the end of line *c* rhymes with a word in the first half of line *d*, thus forming a couplet in *awdl-gywydd* metre, also found throughout St 70. Later *englynion cyrch* regularly have additional internal ornamentation in lines *a* and *b*, as do, for example, the first and third of the three englynion the magician Gwydion sings to the mortally wounded Lleu Llaw Gyffes in eagle's shape in the Fourth Branch of *The Mabinogi* (Mab 105). In the two *englynion cyrch* here, however, there is only the *llwyr-lluosog* alliteration and the rhyme *llwyr-gŵyr* in 32b.

St 70 is the exception that is not an englyn at all. It is rather a string of three seven-syllable couplets in the ancient metre known as *awdl-gywydd*, in which the second lines carry the main rhyme and the end of each first line rhymes with a word in the middle of the second line.

Textual Notes

The Black Book of Carmarthen

At the top of folio 32 a later (15c?) hand has written *Englynnionn y Beddev*. The stanzas themselves begin on the second line of the page (following the last line of the preceding poem), with a small capital E and a large B (1 and 3 lines in height, respectively), both in red ink.

1b. *orddyfnasynt*: MS *ortywnassint*. TJ emends to *tywnassint*.

4b. *yng ngodir Bryn Aren*: P98B *yngwarthaf Bryn Arien* (on top of Bryn Arien).

4c. *Llanfeuno*: P98B: *yn Llanveuno*.

5b. *graeandde*: TJ emends to *graende* to improve the syllable count; Jarman suggests *yn y* can be contracted to *ny*.

10a-b. P98B: *Bedd Panna fab Pyd yngorthir Arfon / [y] dan ei oer weryd* (The grave of Panna ap Pyd in the highlands of Arfon / under its cold earth).

11c. *bedd Cynon*: MS *bet kinon*. TJ deletes *bet* for the syllable count.

19b. *llwrw*: TJ suggests emending the MS *llurv* to [*gor*]*llurv* for the syllable count.

27b. *byddai*: TJ suggest shortening the line to *ny bei gurth breinhin*; B xxii suggests *ni bei gur breinhin*.

28c. *Gwanas Gwŷr*: MS *guanas* with *guir* (= *gwŷr* 'of men/warriors'?) inserted above the line in the same hand. TJ suggests it could be omitted, but the intentional addition, with double insertion marks below the line, is an argument for keeping it.

35c. *gŵr oedd hwnnw*: MS *gur oet hvnnv*. TJ omits *oet hvnnv* for the syllable count, but cf. St P2c.

37c. *hirwynion*: MS *hirguynion*. TJ emends to *hirwyn* for the syllable count.

38c. *Beidog Rudd yw hwn*. MS *beidauc rut yv hun*. TJ omits *yv hun* for the syllable count.

39a. *o Bryden*. MS p²*dein*. The ² over the *p* is a standard abbreviation for *ri*. TJ emends *pridein* to *priden* for the internal rhyme with *unben*. The forms *Prydain* (Britain) and *Prydyn* ('Pictland', 'Scotland', or 'the North'), variously spelled, are often confused in early manuscripts; here the latter is surely meant.

41a. *cnud*. MS *cund*.

42c. *rhwyfenydd ran*. This is the only know instance of *rhwyfenydd* (lord, ruler, prince), from *rhwyfan* (to rule, govern). The translation of *ran* as 'look' follows TJ, who takes *ran* as the lenited form of *gran* (cheek); he also notes that *ran* could be understood as the lenited form of *rhan*, which he renders 'of princely portion'.

45a. *glaw*. MS *glav*. TJ emends to *y glav* to improve the syllable count. Alternatively, the variant of this englyn in the *Red Book* reads *Tom Elwithan neus gwlych glaw* (EWSP 443).

c. *Cynon yno ei gwyno*. MS *Kynon yno i kiniav*. The emendation of *kiniav* to *kuinav* is supported both by the sense and by the reading *gwynaw* in the *Red Book* variant St R5. Might the MS reading indicate a misinterpretation of the penstrokes as the scribe was copying a written text? *Yno* (there) does not appear in the *Red Book*.

46a. MS *Piev y bet hun, Bet hun a hun*. TJ deletes the second *Bet hun* for the syllable count. The manuscript reading, however, is more rhetorically forceful.

47c. *mai*. This could be an old genitive or plural form of *ma* (plain, field) or a proper name; compare *Gwalchmai* (see TYP 369).

49a. MS *Piev y bet hun nid*.

49c. MS *vrthid*. The *Black Book* spelling is reflected in the modernised text, rather than the modern *wrthyt*, in order to retain the rhyme.

52a. *yn yngyrth*. MS *yg kinhen*. TJ suggests the emendation to *yn yngyrth* to provide internal rhyme with *talyrth* and end rhyme with *nyrth/byrth*; he notes that a similar rhyme scheme occurs in St 51 and fifteen other stanzas. *Engyrth/yngyrth* (GPC 'dread, horror, direfulness'; LPBT 'tempests') conveys suitable connotations for this line, similar to those of *cynnen* (contention, strife; battle, conflict).

53c. MS *pen llv wu tra wu y amser* (lit. He was head of a host while his time was). TJ deletes the first *wu* (i.e., *fu* (he was)) to improve the syllable count.

54a. *gwrdd*. MS *gurth*.

55b. *yw hwnnw*. MS *yv hunnv* (that is). TJ deletes *hunnv* for the syllable count.

c. TJ suggests reading *Digonai dda ar arfau* (He accomplished good with arms) to improve the syllable count.

56a. MS *Piev y bet breint*, with *hun bet* added above the line between *bet* and *breint* in different ink.

b. *Llyfni*. MS *lewin*.

c. *ysgeraint*. MS *isscarant*, corrected for the rhyme to *isscereint* in the same hand that corrected 56a.

59c. *i'w*. MS *y* (= *y'y*)

60a. *ei drefred*. MS *y trewrud*. Emend to *y drefred* (homestead); cf. St 25a.

60c. *caffai*. MS *caffei*. TJ emends to *[ef] caffei*.

61c. *Rhi oedd ef*. MS *Ri oet ew*. TJ deletes *oet* for the syllable count.

62b. *gwaywawr rudd*. MS *guawrut*. TJ emends for the syllable count.

64b. *y mae bedd gŵr*. MS *y mae gur*.

66c. *o drais*. MS *ino treis*.

67c. *bradog*. MS *brauc*.

70-73. These four englynion were added to the bottom half of the page in the same hand using a somewhat different orthography. Thomas Jones, consulting with Dr. Hywel D. Emanuel, suggests a date in the second half of the thirteenth century (TJ 98). The different ink indicates a later insertion by the scribe who worked on the *Black Book* over a period of time; the different orthography may indicate either a source in different orthography or a change in the scribe's orthographic practice.

70e. *Garwen*. MS *earrwen*.

71c. *Cyhored*. MS *gyhoret*. TJ points out that the syntax requires the subject should be unlenited.

72b. MS *pieu yr vedgor yssy yma*. TJ, following Sir John Rhŷs, suggests reading *pieu'r vedgor sy yma* to make a seven syllable line.

The Red Book of Hergest

R1. This stanza is irregular (see EWSP 412, 532).

a. *Llyma yma*: Following TJ I have retained the possibly otiose *yma*; Rowland emends to *Llyma* and translates 'Here is' (EWSP 472).

b. *ry seai*: MS *ys ei*. TJ, following Ifor Williams (CLlH 92), emends to *[r]yse[e]i* (would have spread). Rowland suggests emending *tringar* to *trugar*, *ysei* to *ys [a]ei*, and reading 'Here is the grave of a faultless one, merciful (generous) to poets. His fame used to go where he, Pyll, would not have gone even had he lived longer' (EWSP 532).

R2a. *Bedd*. MS *Oed*, with the *O* underdotted for deletion; *Bedh* is written in the margin in a later hand. Ifor Williams suggests that the mistake stems from misreading an old *B* (CLlH 93).

NLW Peniarth MS 98B

P2a. *Bedd Gwaeanwyn*. MS *Bedd y Gwanwyn*. The emendation of *Gwanwyn* to *Gwaeanwyn* is adopted from TJ, who omits *y* from the text; compare the similar emendation of *gwannwyn* to *gwaeannwyn* in CLlH 9.

c. *gŵr oedd ef*: MS *gwr oedd ef*. TJ omits *oedd ef* for the syllable count, but cf. St 35c.

P3a. *Dinlle*. MS *Dinleu*.

c. The line is obscure. The MS *Garanawg* may represent a proper name.

P4a. In the MS *ddinau* is written above *ddiau*. The line is obscure.

c. MS *arwynawl gedawl gredig*. TJ suggests the MS reading is a corruption of *arwynawl kedawl Kredig*.

P5b. *gawr a gwewyr*. IW and TJ emend to *gawr a gwaywawr*.

P9b. *dan*. MS *dan*. TJ emends to *y dan*.

P10b. After *ei* Davies originally wrote *afles*, then crossed it out and wrote *armes*.

c. TJ omits *ef* to give a line of seven syllables.

P11a. After *afon* something has been crossed out. TJ translates 'on a river'.

c. *Rugri*. Originally written *ywgri*, with *Ru* added above the *yw*. TJ notes that the copy of these stanzas in Peniarth MS 111 by John Jones Gellilyfdy (c.1610) reads *Yvgri*.

P14. *ciglef*: MS *Cic len*, with a note above reading (*v.r. leu*); see the note to St P14 above.

P15c. *gwynnofwr*: MS *gwen efwr*. TJ retains the manuscript reading, but adopts in his translation (as here) Lloyd-Jones' suggestion that it is a corruption of *gwynnofwr* (one who causes destruction) (G, s.v. *gwenefwr*).

P16c. TJ suggests inserting *bedd* before *Mabon* to achieve a seven-syllable line; however, the close similarity of this line to W1c suggests that this may not be a scribal omission.

P17a. *anap lleian*: MS *Ann ap lleian*. See the note to this stanza.

P18bc. *ryde… Alun Dyfe[d]*: MS *ryde … Alun Dyfe*.

Wrexham MS 1

W1c. TJ suggests inserting *bedd* before *Gwryd* to achieve a seven-syllable line, but see the note to P16c above.

St 19. The Gamber stream near its source at Gamber Head

St W1. Bryn Beddau, Clocaenog Forest, Clwyd

Abbreviations and Bibliography

AMR   Archiv Melville Richards: *http://www.e-gymraeg.co.uk/enwaulleoedd/amr/ cronfa_en.aspx*

AP   Jones, D. Gwenallt, ed. *Yr Areithiau Pros*. (Cardiff: University of Wales Press, 1934)

AW   *The Arthur of the Welsh*. Rachel Bromwich, A. O. H. Jarman, Brynley F. Roberts, edd. (Cardiff: University of Wales Press, 1991)

B   *Bulletin of the Board of Celtic Studies*

BB   Parry, John Jay. *Brut y Brenhinedd* (Cambridge, Massachusetts: Medieval Academy of America, 1937)

Bleg   Williams, S. J., and J. E. Powell. *Cyfreithiau Hywel Dda*. (Cardiff: University of Wales Press, 1961)

BLl   Evans, J. Gwenogvryn, ed. *The Text of the Book of Llan Dâv*. (Oxford, 1893 [rptd. Aberystwyth: National Library of Wales, 1979])

CA   Williams, Ifor. *Canu Aneirin*. (Cardiff: University of Wales Press, 1961)

CLlH   Williams, Ifor, ed. *Canu Llywarch Hen*. (Cardiff: University of Wales Press, 1953)

CO   Rachel Bromwich and D. Simon Evans, edd. *Culhwch and Olwen*. (Cardiff: University of Wales Press, 1992)

Coflein   *Royal Commission on the Ancient and Historical Monuments of Wales website: http://www.cbhc.gov.uk/*

CT   Bollard, John K., trans. *Companion Tales to The Mabinogi*. (Llandysul: Gomer, 2007)

DP   Owen, George. T*he Description of Penbrokshire*. Henry Owen, ed. (London, 1892)

EWSP   Rowland, Jenny. *Early Welsh Saga Poetry*. (Cambridge: D.S. Brewer, 1990)

G   Lloyd-Jones, J. *Geirfa Barddoniaeth Gynnar Gymraeg*. (Cardiff: University of Wales Press, 1931-63)

GP   Williams, G. J., and E. J. Jones. *Gramadegau'r Penceirddiaid*. (Cardiff: University of Wales Press, 1934)

GPC   *Geiriadur Prifysgol Cymru: A Dictionary of the Welsh Language*. (Cardiff: University of Wales Press, 1950-2002)

HB   John Morris, ed. and trans. *Historia Brittonum in Nennius: British History and the Welsh Annals*. (London: Phillimore, 1980)

HEC   Bede. *History of the English Church and People*. Leo Sherley-Price, trans. (Harmondsworth: Penguin, 1965)

HRB   Geoffrey of Monmouth. *Historia Regum Britanniae A Variant Version*. Jacob Hammer, ed. (Cambridge, Massachusetts: Mediaeval Academy of America, 1951)

HW   Lloyd, J. E. *A History of Wales*. (London: Longman, 1912 [rptd. 1967]).

LlDC   A.O.H. Jarman, ed. *Llyfr Du Caerfyrddin*. (Cardiff: University of Wales Press, 1982)

LlH   Morris-Jones, John, and T.H. Parry-Williams. *Llawysgrif Hendragadredd*. (Cardiff: University of Wales Press, 1933 [rptd. 1971])

LPBT   Haycock, Marged, ed. and trans. *Legendary Poems from the Book of Taliesin*. (Aberystwyth: CMCS, 2007)

Mab   Bollard, John K., trans. *The Mabinogi*. (Llandysul: Gomer, 2006)

NLW   National Library of Wales

P98B   NLW Peniarth MS 98B

PNP   Charles, B. G. *The Place-Names of Pembrokeshire*. (Aberystwyth, 1992)

PT   Williams, Ifor, ed. *The Poems of Taliesin*. (Dublin: Dublin Institute for Advanced Studies, 1968)

RoA   Bollard, John. K. 'Arthur in the Early Welsh Tradition' in *The Romance of Arthur*, Norris J. Lacy and James J. Wilhelm, edd. (London and New York: Routledge, 2013, 9-27)

RoM   Bollard, John K. 'Myrddin in Early Welsh Tradition' in *The Romance of Merlin*, Peter Goodrich, ed. (New York and London: Garland, 1990, 13-54)

RLSD   James, J. W., ed. *Rhigyfarch's Life of St David*. (Cardiff: University of Wales Press, 1967)

SC   *Studia Celtica*

TA   Bollard, John, K., trans. *Tales of Arthur*. (Llandysul: Gomer, 2010)

TJ   Jones, Thomas. 'The Black Book of Carmarthen "Stanzas of the Graves"'. (*Proceedings of the British Academy*, LIII (1968), 97-137)

TYP   Bromwich, Rachel, ed. and trans. *Trioedd Ynys Prydein: The Welsh Triads*, 2nd Ed. (Cardiff: University of Wales Press, 1978)

WCD   Bartrum, Peter C. *A Welsh Classical Dictionary*. (Aberystwyth: National Library of Wales, 1993)

YMT   A. O. H. Jarman, ed. *Ymddiddan Myrddin a Thaliesin*. (Cardiff, 1967)

Baring Gould, S., R. Burnard, and Irvine K. Anderson. 'Exploration of Moel Trigarn'. (*Archaeologica Cambrensis* 1900, 189-211)

Bingley, William. *North Wales; including its Scenery, Antiquities, Customs, and Some Sketches of its Natural History*. (London: Longman, 1804)

Davies, Wendy. *The Llandaff Charters*. (Aberystwyth: National Library of Wales, 1979)

Edwards, Nancy. 'Early-Medieval Inscribed Stones and Stone Sculpture in Wales: Context and Function'. (*Medieval Archaeology*, 45 (2001), 15-39)

Evans, Dafydd Huw. 'An Incident on the River Dee during the Glyn Dŵr Rebellion?' (*Transactions of the Denbighshire Historical Society* 37 (1988), 5-40)

Ford, Patrick K., ed. *Ystoria Taliesin*. (Cardiff: University of Wales Press, 1992)

Ford, Patrick K., trans. *The Mabinogi and Other Welsh Tales*. (Berkeley and Los Angeles: University of California Press: 1977)

Gruffydd, R. Geraint. 'Canu Cadwallon ap Cadfan'. *Astudiaethau ar yr Hengerdd: Studies in Old Welsh Poetry*. Rachel Bromwich and R. Brinley Jones, eds. (Cardiff: University of Wales Press, 1978).

Jarman, A. O. H., ed. and trans. *Aneirin: Y Gododdin*. (Llandysul: Gomer, 1988)

Johnston, Dafydd, ed. and trans. *Iolo Goch: Poems*. (Llandysul: Gomer, 1993)

Koch, John T. *Cunedda, Cynan, Cadwallon, Cynddylan*. (Aberystwyth: University of Wales Centre for Advanced Welsh and Celtic Studies, 2013)

Koch, John T., ed. and trans. *The Gododdin of Aneirin*. (Cardiff: University of Wales Press, 1997)

Livingston, Michael. *The Battle of Brunanburh*. (Exeter: Exeter University Press, 2011)

Lloyd-Jones, J. *Enwau Lleoedd Sir Caernarfon*. (Cardiff: University of Wales Press, 1928)

Sims-Williams, Patrick. 'anfab[2] "illegitimate child", a ghost-word'. (*Bulletin of the Board of Celtic Studies* 18 (1978), 90-93)

Thomson, R. L., ed. *Owein*. (Dublin: Dublin Institute for Advanced Studies, 1968)

William of Malmesbury. *Chronicle of the Kings of England*. J.A. Giles, trans. (London: Henry G. Bohn, 1847)

St 12. Mist in the pass at Bwlch Oerddrws (Camlan)

Index of Personal Names

	Stanza	Page		Stanza	Page
Agen ap Rhugri	P11	57, 105	Cynfael	65	47, 92, 97
Ager	P11	57, 105	Cynfeli	65	47, 97
Airgwl	71	48, 100	Cynon	8, 10, 45, 65, R5, P9	21-2, 38, 47, 52, 57, 70, 88-9, 97, 109-10, 118, 125, 128
Alun Dyfed ap Meigen	25	29, 59, 78-9, 89, 118, 130			
Amir	19	17, 78, 115			
anap lleian	P17	59, 106, 130			
Aron ap Dyfnwyn	59	42, 95, 110	Cynon ap Clydno Eidyn	9, 11	22, 70, 110
Arthur	44	37, 60-1, 69-70, 72, 75, 78, 81, 83-5, 87-8, 91, 96, 99, 106, 109-11, 114-16, 120	Cywryd	1	17, 60, 106, 117
			Dehewaint	58	42, 94
			Disgyrnin Disgyffeddod	P14	57, 105
			Dylan	4, P7, P13	16-7, 56-7, 61-2, 82, 110, 123
Bedwyr	12	22, 72	Dywel ab Erbin	27	31, 79-80
Beidog Rudd ab Emyr Llydaw	36, 37, 38	14, 33-5, 83, 110, 115, 118, 128	Ebediw ap Maelwr	68	48, 98
			Eidal ap Meigen	46, 47	38, 78, 89, 115
			Eiddew ap Meigen	46, 47	38, 78, 89, 92, 115
Beli ap Benlli Gawr	73	50, 101, 117			
Bradwen	62	44, 61, 96	Eiddïwlch the Tall ab Arthan	34	33, 82
Braint	56	41, 92-3			
Brwyno Hir	48	13, 39, 89, 92, 111	Eilinwy	50	39, 91
			Einion ap Cunedda	72	50, 100, 110
Caw	1	17, 60-1, 110, 117	Eirinfedd	R4	52, 104, 118
			Elchwith	45	38, 70, 88-9, 97, 118
Ceri Cleddyf Hir	5	18, 62, 110, 112, 118	Elffin	42, 43	36, 85, 87, 120, 122
Cerwyd	1	17, 60, 117			
Coel ap Cynfelyn	57	41, 94	Elidir Mwynfawr	P15	57, 105, 110
Credig	P4	54, 104	Elsner ap Nêr	53	40, 91, 118
Cyhored	71	48, 100, 129	Elwydd	64	46, 89, 97
Cynddilig ap Corcnud	41	36, 85	Elwyddan	R5	52, 88-9, 97
Cynddylan	15	24, 61, 71, 76	Epynt	26	29, 79, 95, 108, 113

	Stanza	*Page*		*Stanza*	*Page*
Erbin	31	31-2, 78-80, 82	Llofan Llawygyn	P6	54, 82, 105
Ffyrnfael Hael ab Hywlydd	33, P1	33, 54, 82, 111	Llorien	R2	52, 103
			Lluosgar	36	33, 83
Garwen ferch Hennin	70	48, 98-100, 111, 129	Llwch Llawengin	31	32, 82, 105, 118
			Llwyd Llednais	66	47, 98, 110, 123
Gwaeanwyn	P2	54, 104, 130	Llwyddog ap Lliwelydd	32	32, 82
Gwalchmai	8	21, 69-70, 110, 114, 128	Llygedwy ap Llywarch	R3	52, 103
			Llywy	70	48, 98-100
Gwallog Hir	7	20, 67-8, 110, 120	mab Osfran	12	22, 72, 109
			Mabon ap Mydron Glau	P16	58, 81, 105-6, 130
Gwell	R2	52, 103			
Gwên	3	17, 61, 81	Madog	20, 63	27, 45, 52, 78, 96, 116
Gwên ab Llywarch Hen	16	26, 76-7, 80			
Gwgon Red-Sword	44	37, 88, 114	Madog ap Gwyn	21	28, 78
Gwrgi	28	31, 80, 110-11	March	44	37, 87, 114
Gwriad	3	17, 61	Meigen ap Rhun	17, 18, 19	26-7, 29, 38, 78-9, 89, 110-11, 115, 118
Gwrien	2, 3, 32	17, 32, 61, 82			
Gwrtheyrn Gwrthenau	40	35, 83-5, 106, 110			
Gwryd ap Gwryd Glau	W1	59, 106, 130	Meilyr ap Brwyn	20, 23	27-8, 78, 116
Gwydion ap Dôn	P3	54, 62, 104, 123, 126	Môr Mawrhydig ap Peredur Penweddig	20, 22	27-8, 78, 116
Gwythur	44	37, 87-8, 114	Morial	2	17, 61
Gyrthmwl	39	35, 84, 110	Morien	2	17, 61, 96
Henyn Henben	71	48, 99-100, 111	Myrddin Emrys	P17	59, 106
Llachar	54	40, 91	Omni	36	33
Llachar ap Rhun	51	39, 79, 91, 118	Owain	14	24, 76, 109, 112
Llawr	28	31, 52, 80, 111	Owain ab Urien	13	24, 70, 74-5, 88, 105, 109-10, 112, 114, 118, 125
Lledin	70	48, 98-9, 111			
Llemenig	50	39, 90-1			
Lleu Llaw Gyffes	35, P10	33, 57, 62, 82-3, 104, 110, 123, 126	Panna fab Pyd	P9	57, 71, 76, 128
			Pryderi	7	20, 66, 110, 113, 123
Llia Gwyddel	26	29, 79, 118			
Llofan Llaw Ddifo	P7, P8	56-7, 104-5	Pyll	R1	52, 129
Llofan Llaw Estrawn	P5	54	Rhiogan	61	44, 96

	Stanza	*Page*
Rhufawn	42, 43	36, 87, 118
Rhun	61	44, 96, 109
Rhun	70	48, 96, 99, 105, 109, 111
Rhun ab Alun Dyfed	24, P18	29, 59, 79, 118
Rhun ap Pyd	10	22, 71, 118
Rhwyf ap Rhygenau	55	41, 92
Rhydderch Hael	13	24, 75, 105, 110-11
Sanant	70	48, 98-9, 111
Sawyl	R2	52, 103
Seithennin	6	19, 64-5
Siôn Syberw	67	47, 96, 98
Silidd Dywal	50	39, 90
Taflogau ap Lludd	60	42, 92, 95, 114
Talan Thrusting Brow	52	40, 91, 111
teulu Oeth ac Anoeth	30	32, 81-2
Tydai Tad Awen	4, P13	17, 57, 61-2
Urien	21	28, 76, 78, 104-5, 110, 119, 125

St 26. Mynydd Epynt, looking to the Brecon Beacons

St 26. Dyffryn Ardudwy burial chambers

Index of Place Names

	Stanza	Page		Stanza	Page
Aber Bangori	P11	57, 105	Gwanas Gwŷr	28	31, 81, 111, 128
Aber Gwenoli	7	20, 66, 113, 123	Gwernin bre	50	39, 91
Abererch	13	24, 75	Gwynasedd	39	35, 84
Ardudwy	26	29-30, 79	Heneglwys	5	18, 62, 112
Arfon	P9	57, 60-1, 71, 83, 92, 96-7, 123, 128	Hirerw	67	47, 98
			Hirfynydd	32	32, 82
			Hirwaun	59	42, 95
Brycheiniog	23	28, 97	Llam y Bwch	R2	52, 103
Bryn Arien	4, P13	17, 57, 61-2, 128	Llanbadarn	8	14, 21, 70, 112
			Llanelwy	50	39, 91, 112
Bryn Beddau	W1	59, 106	Llanfeuno	4, P7, P13	17, 56-7, 62-3, 112, 123, 128
Caeo	27	31, 80			
Caer Genedr	6	19, 65-6	Llanforfael	13	24, 75, 112, 118
Camlan	12	22, 60, 72	Llangollen	R2	52-3, 103
Carrog	7	20, 67	Llanhiledd	14	24-5, 76, 112
Cefn Celfi	65	47, 97	Llifon	P2	54, 104
Celli Friafael	39	35, 84	Lliw	39	35, 84, 91
Cemais	66	47, 98, 109	Lloegr	16	26, 74, 76-7, 120
Cerddennin	31	32, 82			
Ceri	36	33, 83	Llwchwr	39	35, 84
Clewaint	58	42, 94	Llyfni	56, P2	41, 54, 92, 104, 129
Clun Cain	51	39, 91			
Corbre	5	18, 62, 112	Machawy	37, 38	34-5, 83-4, 103, 118
Defeillon	P3	54, 104			
Dinorben	71	48, 100-02	Maes Maoddyn	R4, R5	52, 104, 125
Dyar	54	40, 91	Maes Mawr	73	50-1, 101
Dyfed	71	48, 66, 79-80, 100, 118	Maes Meueddog	45	38, 104
			Mathafarn	58	42, 94
Edrywy	50	39, 90	Menai	P7, P8	56-7
Eifionydd	64	46, 96-7	Meweddus	P15	57, 105
Emrais	P17	59	Morfa Dinlle	P3	12-3, 20, 54-5, 104, 123
Ergryd	10	22, 71			
Gefel	26	29, 79, 113	Morfa, y	70	48-9, 98-101, 111
Gwanas	29, 30	32, 81, 111			

	Stanza	*Page*
Nantlle	P16	58, 83, 105-6
Pant Gwyn Gwynionog	20	27, 78
Pennant Twrch	34	33, 82
Penweddig	22	28, 78
Peryddon	8	14, 21, 70, 114
Prydain, -ein, -en, -yn	39, 72	35, 60, 61, 85, 100, 120, 128
Rheon Rhyd	10, P9	22, 57, 71
Rhiw Lyfnaw	36	33, 83
Rhiw Felen	R2	52-3, 103
Rhyd Brydw	36	33, 83
Rhyd Faen-ced	24	29, 79, 118
Rhyd Gynan	71	48, 100
Rhyd y Garwfaen	P18	59
Rhydau, y	55	41, 92
Rhuddnant	61	44, 95-6
Tafwy	54	40, 92
Tryfan	12	22-3, 58, 72-3
Ystyfachau	40	35, 85

Sts 28-30. Rhos Gwanas